DUETS

A Comedy in Four Acts

by Peter Quilter

samuelfrench.co.uk

FOR AMATEUR PRODUCTION ENQUIRIES

UNITED KINGDOM AND WORLD
EXCLUDING NORTH AMERICA
plays@samuelfrench.co.uk
020 7255 4302/01

Each title is subject to availability from Samuel French,
depending upon country of performance.

THINKING ABOUT PERFORMING A SHOW?

There are thousands of plays and musicals available to perform from Samuel French right now, and applying for a licence is easier and more affordable than you might think

---

From classic plays to brand new musicals, from monologues to epic dramas, there are shows for everyone.

Plays and musicals are protected by copyright law, so if you want to perform them, the first thing you'll need is a licence. This simple process helps support the playwright by ensuring they get paid for their work and means that you'll have the documents you need to stage the show in public.

Not all our shows are available to perform all the time, so it's important to check and apply for a licence before you start rehearsals or commit to doing the show.

LEARN MORE & FIND THOUSANDS OF SHOWS

Browse our full range of plays and musicals, and find out more about how to license a show
www.samuelfrench.co.uk/perform

Talk to the friendly experts in our Licensing team for advice on choosing a show and help with licensing
plays@samuelfrench.co.uk   020 7387 9373

Acting Editions

BORN TO PERFORM

Playscripts designed from the ground up to work the way you do in rehearsal, performance and study

---

Larger, clearer text for easier reading

Wider margins for notes

Performance features such as character and props
lists, sound and lighting cues, and more

+ CHOOSE A SIZE AND STYLE TO SUIT YOU

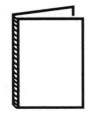

STANDARD EDITION

Our regular
paperback book at
our regular size

SPIRAL-BOUND EDITION

The same size
as the Standard
Edition, but with a
sturdy, easy-to-fold,
easy-to-hold
spiral-bound spine

LARGE EDITION

A4 size and spiral
bound, with larger text
and a blank page for
notes opposite every
page of text – perfect
for technical and
directing use

LEARN MORE | **samuelfrench.co.uk/actingeditions**

Other plays by PETER QUILTER
published and licensed by Samuel French

4000 Days

The Actress

Boyband

Curtain Up!

Glorious!

Just The Ticket

The Nightingales

Saving Jason

FIND PERFECT PLAYS TO PERFORM AT
www.samuelfrench.co.uk/perform

MUSIC USE NOTE

IMPORTANT BILLING AND CREDIT REQUIREMENTS

Duets had its USA premiere at the Aurora Theatre in Georgia, and its European premiere at the Cultural Centre in Vilnius, Lithuania

The play was then re-structured and presented in its current form for the first time at the Ensemble Theatre in Sydney, Australia. The premiere took place on 20th August 2009, featuring actors Barry Creyton and Noeline Brown, and was directed by Sandra Bates.

CHARACTERS

Duet I - Blind Date	WENDY, JONATHAN
Duet II - Secretarial Skills	JANET, BARRIE
Duet III - The Holiday	SHELLEY, BOBBY
Duet IV - The Bride-To-Be	ANGELA, TOBY

The setting throughout is the living room of an apartment

Time: the present

PRODUCTION NOTES

Duets is comprised of four short plays, each with two characters. Companies can present the play using eight performers (4f, 4m) or can choose to double-up some of the roles (4f, 2m, etc).

There is one set – the living room of an apartment – some of the features and props of which will change for each of the four plays. The apartment has a door leading outside, a second door to the bedroom, and a window. There is a sofa, chairs, a cabinet of glasses and drinks, a full length mirror and a coffee table plus a phone, etc. There is an open plan kitchen which forms part of the living room. There are several features which change for each play – a vase of flowers, a painting on the wall, a large ornament, a plant, a lamp, the floor rug, the sofa cover – these should be changed each time to match the personality of the characters and location.

It is suggested that the characters of Duet II are American and that the characters of Duet IV are British. But companies should feel flexible about this if they don't want to be tied to a particular accent.

Scene changes should happen as quickly as possible and a famous song duet, subject to separate copyright clearance, should be heard in each scene change. Companies are free to make their own choice of music for these changes. But the songs should always be a duet between two singers and reflect in some way the themes of the plays. Larger scale productions might choose to show videos of these song duets in the scene changes, or perhaps even have live singers and a piano.

Peter Quilter

Peter Quilter would like to dedicate
this play to

Sandra Bates

and

Francisco Martín Hernández

and

Juan Carlos Martín Medina

ACT I

Duet I – Blind Date

Both characters in the play are in their late fifties or older and have dressed nicely for a first date—but neither has good taste. WENDY *wears glasses.* JONATHAN *wears a ginger toupée.*

Lights rise on the empty apartment.

A knock at the door. JONATHAN *enters from the bedroom, checks his appearance, then opens the door.* WENDY *stands beyond the doorway. She is wearing a coat, and carrying a dating magazine and a huge block of cheese.*

JONATHAN Are you Wendy? "Fifty-three, brunette, medium build, glasses" ...? *(Adjust this description to match the actress playing the role)*

WENDY I am. Are you Jonathan— *(Reading from an entry in a dating magazine)* "Tall, slim, olive skinned...thirty-seven?!"

JONATHAN *strikes a youthful pose, despite the description being clearly a couple of decades short.*

JONATHAN I am.

WENDY Oh.

JONATHAN I'm afraid the "olive skin" has faded a little. At the time of writing the description, I'd just come back from Crete. A delightful place, I did enjoy myself—though travelling on your own is never quite the same, is it? You have the freedom, of course, the liberty to do whatever you want and whenever you please—and you see the most marvellous things. But then there's nobody to witness these marvels and you go back to your room with no evidence that you were there at all and was there indeed much point as there's nobody to discuss it with. And suddenly the freedom isn't half so desirable and you wonder if you might have been better off at home watching National Geographic and making one of those trifles that comes in a packet. I've just realised you're still standing in the doorway. I'm so sorry—do come in.

WENDY *enters the room; nervously.*

I do tend to just talk in these situations. Only at the beginning—eventually I do shut up. If not, please feel free to hit me across the head with a large saucepan. Otherwise I'll just keep yapping for no reason at all—much like I am now... Can I take your coat, your magazine and your...block of cheese?

WENDY *(having momentarily forgotten about the huge block of cheese in her hand)* Oh yes! That's for you. *(Handing it to him, along with her coat and the magazine)* Have some cheese.

JONATHAN Oh. Well—that's—well, there you go—that's left me speechless.

WENDY *(nervously)* ...Well, I don't drink, you see. Not generally. So I thought it would be silly to bring wine, because then you'd feel awkward about opening it just for yourself. Plus I'd buy the wrong kind and we'd end up with some terrible bottle of Spanish plonk. And I couldn't bring juice or mineral water because you'd think me a bit strange.

JONATHAN I wouldn't dream of thinking you strange. At least, not before I'd got to know you.

WENDY The thing is—that you men have it so much easier, don't you? You can turn up with flowers or chocolates and you can't go wrong there. But what does a woman bring to a man's house? So I thought—what do men like? Cheese! Men like cheese. So I brought cheese... Do you like cheese?

JONATHAN I love cheese.

WENDY Oh good! Well—there you are. Now you have cheese. Lots and lots. Enough to feed a small country.

JONATHAN Yes. *(Smelling it)* I'll pop it in the fridge.

WENDY Yes, you should. It's been on the bus.

> **JONATHAN** *heads for the fridge.*

It's goat's.

JONATHAN Oh. Will he want it back?

WENDY No—I mean it's made with milk from a goat, it's goat's cheese... Or were you making a joke?

JONATHAN Just a little one.

WENDY Oh, yes. *(She forces a laugh)*

JONATHAN It was rather a feeble attempt at humour.

WENDY No, no. I shall really laugh later in bed. *(Suddenly realising)* Oh, no! I didn't mean to suggest—

JONATHAN I hope not. I was thinking—now steady on there!

WENDY Oh, dear!

JONATHAN Let's get to know each other first.

WENDY Yes!

> *They both force a laugh. Which is followed by total silence.*

JONATHAN Do have a seat. *(He hangs up her coat, but still has the magazine in his hand)*

> **WENDY** *sits down.*

Terrible, really, these magazines, aren't they?

WENDY Oh—yes.

JONATHAN Not that I'm not glad that we've had this chance to meet. I just mean the—putting the advert in—it's such a—

WENDY Yes.

JONATHAN You feel a bit pathetic, don't you? Advertising yourself. It's like putting a billboard outside in your front garden— "Wife needed! Apply within!"

WENDY But it works sometimes—gets results.

JONATHAN Yes—well, here *we* are. *(Flicking through the magazine)* ...And of course—we're not the worst, are we? I mean—some of these... *(Reading one of the adverts)* "Ex-army bald-headed man looking for companion to share love of rattle snakes and Peruvian cinema."

WENDY *forces a chuckle.*

(he reads another) ... "Seventy year-old man seeks female... to start a family!"

WENDY No!

JONATHAN Oh yes! *(Showing her the magazine)* It's right there next to the advert for Viagra.

WENDY He should be their spokesman.

JONATHAN He should. *(He forces a chuckle)*

WENDY *(taking the magazine and reading out another advert)* "Belgian man into scuba diving, crochet, alligators, leather bondage, fantasy role play, handcuffs, Bavarian cookery and spanking...seeks similar...!"

They both laugh at this, less forced this time.

JONATHAN How awful!

WENDY Yes—*Bavarian* cookery...!

JONATHAN He sounds shocking.

WENDY Yes. That's why we only went out the one time... Joking!

JONATHAN Ah! You got me back... Can I get you some—erm, juice? Or—cheese?

WENDY Orange juice?

JONATHAN I think we can manage that.

WENDY Perfect. Thank you.

JONATHAN *returns to the kitchen and pours two glasses of orange juice.*

It was very understanding of you to agree to just a fifteen minute chat, before—well...rather than jumping straight into dinner.

JONATHAN It struck me as perfectly sensible. Jumping into dinner can be very messy. And you don't always want a full dinner with a stranger, do you? You don't know whether it's going to be—

WENDY —And sometimes you know by mid-way through the appetiser that it's not right.

JONATHAN —And you're just stuck there through the main course and everything.

WENDY It can be horrible.

JONATHAN I know. And expensive.

WENDY Yes. You have a horrible, embarrassing meal—and then you have to pay for it.

JONATHAN I always hate that moment when one of you has to be brave enough to ask, "Shall we have dessert?" You might as well just ask, "Do you find me remotely attractive, or shall we throw the towel in now?" "Yes" to the pudding means "Yes, you're attractive". "No, I'm full up" means "I want to get the hell out of here and you're a hideous freak of nature." *(He gives her the orange juice)*

WENDY You're not.

JONATHAN Not?

WENDY A hideous freak of nature.

JONATHAN Oh...thank you... That might be the worst compliment I've ever had.

WENDY Oh dear...

JONATHAN Oh well...

They drink their juice.

WENDY ...But this is better, I think. Just meet and have a quick chat and see if...see if we want to have dinner...some other time.

JONATHAN At least that way, we know whether dessert is likely to be on the cards or not.

WENDY My thoughts exactly. I'm so glad you agree. Thank you for inviting me over.

JONATHAN Not at all.

WENDY We can ignore worrying about the bigger picture and just have a good old conversation.

JONATHAN Yes—a bloody good chat.

Silence. They drink more juice. **JONATHAN** *finishes his and returns to the kitchen to pour himself some more.*

WENDY Have you lived here long?

JONATHAN A few years.

WENDY It's very nice.

JONATHAN It serves its purpose. I'd like somewhere with a garden really. Do you like gardening?

WENDY I don't have the patience. It all happens far too slowly for me. When you get to my age, you want everything to get a move on. You can wait for *years* for a plant to flower. They say it helps if you to talk to them, to give positive energy. But I just end up screaming, "Hurry up and grow you bastards!" which isn't very positive at all. Sorry—I didn't mean to swear.

JONATHAN No, don't apologise. I swear all the time. Particularly when my neighbour starts playing music at two in the morning. He likes military band marches. I'm not sure if he's trying to relax or planning an invasion. My language gets very colourful. But I try and curb my tongue with the ladies. At least until they've got to know me better. Then you can just be yourself, can't you? If it ever gets that far which it generally doesn't. But we keep trying. Love is out there somewhere.

WENDY Oh yes. But it hides itself very well, doesn't it? ...Have you met lots of women? —From the magazine, I mean...

JONATHAN A few, yes. I used to always look for the vivacious ones, the young and beautiful ones. But it never worked out... So I thought I'd give you a try. *(Realising)* ...Which is not to say you're not beautiful yourself—you're extremely—fetching.

WENDY I wish I hadn't worn my glasses. I think I look better these days with my contact lenses. But I'd said in the description that I had glasses and I didn't want to be inaccurate.

JONATHAN No—it's important that the descriptions are precise.

WENDY Yes... Yours says "thirty-seven years old"...?

JONATHAN Aha. *(Looking at her and realising she is unconvinced)* ...That's a printing error of course, it's not what I wrote on the form. Bloody annoying. It should say— *(Thinking for a moment)* ...forty-seven.

WENDY Should it?

JONATHAN ...My mother used to say that you're as old as how you feel.

WENDY Then I must be a hundred and ten.

JONATHAN Well, you don't look it.

WENDY ...Thank you. Though I think that's the worst compliment *I've* ever had...

They both share a chuckle at this.

(continuing to wander; finding a photo of **JONATHAN** *taken on holiday)* ...This looks a nice place.

JONATHAN Yes, that's the Canary Islands. Tenerife.

WENDY Tenerife? Don't they have a volcano?

JONATHAN That's right—in the middle somewhere.

WENDY It looks like the picture is just half of a complete photo. There's a hand round your waist but nobody else there with you.

JONATHAN The lone hand belonged to my fiancée. I had the rest of her chopped out. I have entire photo albums filled with half-torn images like that.

WENDY I suppose it's difficult to know if you should keep the memory as it is or—edit it.

JONATHAN I just prefer to keep the memory of the holiday. I liked the holiday. I think it would be wrong to erase the whole fortnight... Ironically, my fiancée liked the holiday too. Particularly the time she spent with our concierge Sergio. She liked it so much, she never left.

WENDY Oh... So, as we speak, she might actually be *at* the volcano.

JONATHAN Yes. Or preferably—*in* it.

WENDY I'm sorry that happened to you.

JONATHAN Thank you. I'm sorry too. She obviously wasn't "the one".

WENDY I sometimes think I'm not looking for "the one". I'm just looking for "anyone".

JONATHAN I can't believe that's true. I'm sure you'd make any man very happy. And he'd never be short of cheese!

WENDY That's my problem with men. They're all after my gorgonzola...!

JONATHAN *(laughing heartily at this)* You know, you can be very funny.

WENDY Yes—no wonder I'm alone. Nobody wants a funny lady.

JONATHAN Have you not ever been engaged yourself then?

WENDY Actually, yes. Twice. In my pre-funny days. The first engagement just drifted away. But I married my second fiancé.

JONATHAN What was he like?

WENDY His name was Alan. Worked in computer software, played golf. Unusually, I suppose, he was a strict vegetarian. No meat, no fish, no eggs, no honey.

JONATHAN No honey?

WENDY It exploits the bees.

JONATHAN I see.

WENDY The wedding reception was problematic, because he wouldn't have any animal products at the buffet. So it was all mushroom paste and sautéed zucchini. There was nothing that looked edible. The first toast was to "absent friends" and the second one to "absent food". A lot of people left early when word got out there was a Burger King in the next village. At first, I didn't really mind living on a strictly vegetarian diet. Though it amazed me that you could put different combinations of vegetables, pulses and spices into a blender and the result always came out looking and tasting like an old pond. It's silly really because I probably didn't even need to become vegetarian. But he didn't eat meat, so I didn't eat meat. He played golf on a Sunday, so I played golf on a Sunday. He liked jazz, so I liked jazz. It's as though he was some giant machine that sucked away my personality. He was a big blonde Hoover. And it's a shame because I had very high hopes. Which is a mistake, of course. The higher you put your hopes, the more it hurts when you fall down onto your arse... Sorry—there I go again.

JONATHAN No, I thought it was perfectly phrased and summed up the experience with great clarity. Here's to us and our bruised backsides. *(He raises his glass in a toast)*

WENDY *does the same.*

Can I make your juice a bit more interesting? A splash of lemonade, or perhaps—a tiny drop of vodka...?

WENDY Vodka? Well...a little drop, then. But only a tiny, tiny bit.

JONATHAN OK. *(Taking her glass)* You just tell me how much. *(He heads into the kitchen and locates the vodka bottle)*

WENDY *follows to stand nearby.*

Here we are. Smirnoff—direct from Russia...via Tesco. So— just say when.

JONATHAN *upturns the bottle to start pouring but is stopped by* WENDY's *gestures to be less generous. Each tiny movement of the bottle is met with a reaction even though no liquid has actually come out of it yet. Eventually, the tiniest of dribbles plops into the glass and* WENDY *stops him there.*

WENDY That's it! Thank you.

JONATHAN I'm not sure you got any.

WENDY I don't want to get paralytic.

JONATHAN No danger of that.

WENDY Do please have some yourself.

JONATHAN I'm fine. *(Half whispered)* I had some earlier. *(Handing over her drink)* ...To build up courage.

WENDY For me?

JONATHAN I get a bit nervous around the female of the species.

WENDY Why?

JONATHAN Oh, I'm not sure. I just get a bit self-conscious, I suppose. Nobody ever teaches you what you're supposed to do on a date. They make you take lessons for a dozen weeks before you can drive a car, but we go off on these trial relationships with no skills and no map.

WENDY And no safety belt.

JONATHAN Precisely. Somebody's bound to get hurt. I think the hardest thing is that with female company—well, we just never know what you're thinking.

WENDY We don't know what you're thinking either.

JONATHAN Oh, but we're not thinking of anything. No—put us out on a date with an attractive woman and a great fog descends. The brain goes into auto-pilot. So we just take it one pointless sentence at a time and hope for the best. Also, I personally try not to reveal too much at those first dinners, which I suppose keeps me quiet after my inevitable initial bout of yabbering. I don't like somebody to know everything about me in the first ten minutes. One likes to have a little air of mystery... Not that I'm secretive or have anything to hide. There's nothing in my past to be ashamed of.

WENDY I'm sure.

JONATHAN On the contrary, I think—well, there are things I've done which might be regarded as—quite colourful.

WENDY Oh good. What things exactly?

JONATHAN I've travelled very widely. I've enjoyed the arts. I was—yes, I was a volunteer fireman for several weeks...till I burnt my finger. And—I, erm— *(He gets stuck for a moment)* —Oh yes—I won second prize in a dancing competition!

WENDY You did?

JONATHAN Yes, when I was in my twenties back in nineteen-seventy— *(Suddenly correcting himself)* —in erm, nineteen-eighty—ninety—in erm. Back in...my youth—I have a trophy! *(Dashing to a cabinet and carefully extracting the trophy from amongst assorted decanters and glasses)* It's right here... That's it. *(He shows it to* **WENDY***)*

WENDY How exciting. *(Reading the plaque)* Oh— "Ballroom Dancing" —That's quite an unusual thing for a young man to have been involved in.

JONATHAN It happened by accident. I worked in a shop and the owner was a great expert at all that—waltzes and polkas and everything. He had this weekly class and I went along just for a laugh, really. Or perhaps because I was intrigued. And he taught me a few steps, a few moves and—I liked it. There were lots of elderly ladies there and I was a young chap, of course, so I became the object of their desires. I was flattered by the attention. It's always nice to be the youngest man in the room—any room. So—I became a regular and eventually I took part in a local competition and—

WENDY You came second.

JONATHAN I did. It was only a small local thing.

WENDY What a shame you didn't get first prize. I'm sure you deserved it.

JONATHAN No, no, I—actually—yes. I really should have won. Everybody said so. But I knew deep down that I wasn't going to win. You know generally who's going to get the prize. The same old, same old. So, I knew that big glorious bugger of a trophy would not be mine. I remember sitting in my seat during the ceremony dinner and thinking, "Just enjoy it". And I did. I sat and ate my slice of pie and merrily chatted with the other dancers. The various speeches came and went, and when they came to the prizes, I sat there completely content and relaxed, and then in those very final seconds, when they were opening the envelope—suddenly I wanted to win. I wanted to *win*—more than I'd wanted anything in the world. I wanted that huge gleaming trophy in my hands and I thought in those few seconds that it could be mine—and all eyes on me. My moment...but it wasn't. And because I had let my guard down in those final seconds, I felt a great shudder of disappointment and my whole body deflated like an overbaked soufflé. I went up and collected *second* prize— "runner up" —and then I had to stand there like a lemon and congratulate some other person who didn't desire that award half as much as I did. Who didn't, in that moment, want it as much as I wanted it. As I needed it...

WENDY Oh...

JONATHAN Yes, my thoughts exactly.

WENDY But you did very well. You got this nice little second trophy.

JONATHAN Nobody wants to be a bridesmaid. We all want to be the bride.

WENDY Yes, that *is* true. If you *had* won the big trophy, where would you have put it? In the cabinet?

JONATHAN No... In the toilet, naturally. As though it meant nothing... The only problem with putting it in the loo is that you spend the entire evening desperate for your guests to go and have a pee, so they can see it. You catch yourself spiking their syllabub with laxatives. So you might just as well plonk it in the middle of the room and have done with it.

WENDY *(gesturing to centre of the room)* Right there.

JONATHAN Right there.

They stare for a moment at an empty space at the centre of the room.

WENDY It must be good to be a winner. It's not something everyone gets to experience. I never won anything. Not even "runner up". But I keep trying. I could do with some guidance I think—a few lessons.

JONATHAN Dance lessons?

WENDY I sort of meant life lessons, but...learning to dance might be a good idea too.

JONATHAN If you like—I could... I could show you.

WENDY What—now? Here? No, I don't see how that would—I mean, you're obviously very good, but...that would be a bit ridiculous, wouldn't it? There isn't even any music.

JONATHAN *claps his hands loudly twice and this sound automatically turns on his music system. It begins to play Charles Aznavour singing* **"DANCE IN THE OLD FASHIONED WAY"**. *He waits for her to make a move.*

(feeling uncomfortable) I'm sorry, Jonathan, I don't think—

JONATHAN *(clapping his hands twice again and making the music stop)* That's fine. Sorry—it was only a thought. *(He takes the trophy and puts it back in or near the cabinet)*

WENDY ...And it was a lovely thought. But the music started so quickly, I was a bit—

JONATHAN It's an automated system. You just clap your hands.

WENDY Yes I saw that. How clever.

JONATHAN Sorry if it took you by surprise.

WENDY No, it wasn't that—I think I—I didn't feel comfortable all of a sudden.

JONATHAN That's quite understandable—don't give it another thought. You must have wondered if I was about to whisk you around the floor for hours. I was only intending to show you a few moves.

WENDY I realise that. It wasn't that I was— Oh, it's me being silly as usual. No harm in being shown a few dance moves. That would be fun, I'm sure.

JONATHAN *claps his hands again and the music re-starts.*

No, no! I didn't mean that I'd changed my— *(Clapping her hands twice this time to stop the music)* Oh—it works with my hands too! Sorry—that was rude of me, stopping the— Oh, Jonathan, I— Oh dear, I feel so bad that I did that.

JONATHAN It's fine, it's fine. *(He turns away)*

WENDY Please start the music again.

JONATHAN Shall we just sit down and have some more juice?

WENDY Yes.

> *He takes her glass and heads back towards the kitchen.*

> ...No. *(Clapping her hands twice again and re-starting the music)*

JONATHAN *(being stopped in his tracks; speaking loudly over the music)* I thought you wanted juice.

WENDY *(yelling back)* I don't know what I want. Why do you think I'm single?

> **JONATHAN** *shakes his head in confusion but looks at her and they share a little smile. He puts the drinks down and walks back to her. He holds his arms out towards her and she takes hold of one hand. He puts the other hand—gently and respectfully—around her waist. He then walks her through a few simple dance steps in time with the music. She picks up the steps quickly and they dance to the song. Occasionally, she loses the rhythm or treads on his toes. He responds to this with an "ouch!" but they make it part of the fun. The dance continues for a little while, until it is interrupted by the phone ringing in the apartment.*

WENDY That's your phone ringing.

JONATHAN It doesn't matter.

WENDY Don't you want to get it?

JONATHAN It's only— *(They stop dancing)* Yes, I'll just—

> *They both clap hands simultaneously and the music stops and starts and stops again amidst the confusing barrage of claps.* **JONATHAN** *crosses the room and answers the phone. He knows who it is without asking.*

(into the phone) Hi, Paul... No it's fine... Yes... Thanks anyway. *(He hangs up the phone)*

WENDY Oh. Nothing important, then?

JONATHAN No, it was just my—erm... I have a confession to make. That was actually my friend, Paul, who lives upstairs. Whenever I have one of these blind dates—I ask him to give me a call after about fifteen minutes. In case I need an excuse to leave.

WENDY I see...

JONATHAN It's—a little embarrassing. But I thought it best to tell you the truth. I hear a lot of people who advertise in the magazine make similar arrangements. But nonetheless... Sorry.

WENDY That's all right. I can understand that, I suppose. *(Her mobile now starts to loudly ring. She is somewhat horrified by the timing of it and looks at her watch. She takes out the mobile and cancels the call without even looking at it)*

JONATHAN Do you have a "Paul" too?

WENDY Paul*ine*, funnily enough...

JONATHAN We *are* a couple of lost causes, aren't we?

WENDY It's terrible, isn't it? But after five or six bad dates, you start to become strategic. What do you tell them?

JONATHAN Who?

WENDY The ladies. What's the reason you give for having to leave?

JONATHAN I'm generally a Doctor—and I have to rush to the hospital over an emergency *liver* situation.

WENDY Oh that's very inventive. I usually just kill off a relative. I feel a bit guilty sometimes—you know, pretending that some member of the family has just died horribly. But if you think about it hard enough, there's usually some cousin you're happy to bury every Saturday.

JONATHAN *(thinking for a moment)* ...Would you have left?

WENDY What?

JONATHAN ...Had we gone to dinner. And Pauline phoned. Would you have left...?

WENDY No, I wouldn't.

JONATHAN I'm pleased to hear that. *(He notices his trophy and picks it up to carry back to the cabinet)*

WENDY *(continuing)* ...I'd have even stayed for dessert...and coffee.

This makes **JONATHAN** *halt in his movements for a moment.*

JONATHAN *(placing the trophy and closing the cabinet)* Wendy—

WENDY Yes?

JONATHAN Would you consider going for dinner? Now I mean— have dinner...tonight? Is that something you might—ponder over? Would you...?

WENDY *Only*—if you ask me.

JONATHAN Good! Well, consider it asked. We'll go for dinner. Yes— Thank you.

They seem about to kiss each other but it becomes complicated and they somehow end up shaking hands.

WENDY Well, this has gone unexpectedly well, hasn't it? We've only known each other fifteen minutes and we're already shaking hands.

JONATHAN What sort of food do you like to eat?

WENDY Anything that's been shot and killed.

JONATHAN I know just the place. Blood everywhere.

WENDY That sounds perfect. Is it romantic?

JONATHAN Not at the moment. But let's see what we can do once we get there... I'll get my wallet.

WENDY Don't bring too much—we'll be splitting the bill.

JONATHAN Oh—I normally like to pay.

WENDY Men don't pay anymore. You're still stuck in the fifties— *(Correcting herself)* —sixties—seventies—eighties! *(She turns away in embarassment, her hands covering her face)*

JONATHAN *(collecting* **WENDY**'s *coat and his jacket and checking he has his wallet)* You've no doubt realised I'm not even *forty*-seven.

WENDY And I'm not actually a brunette... But who cares what it says on the tin...

JONATHAN *crosses the room, hands her the coat and slips his jacket on.*

JONATHAN *(spotting the dating magazine nearby and picking it up)* We should bring this with us. Have a good laugh at the adverts by all those desperate people. *(Looking at the magazine)* ...We're not desperate, are we?

WENDY No. We're hopeful. I tried desperate and I didn't like it.

JONATHAN Whatever happens—it's really been very nice to meet you.

WENDY You too.

JONATHAN Wouldn't it be wonderful if neither of us ever had to go through all this again?

WENDY Oh, yes. Oh—yes. *(Opening the door)* ...Do you want to lead the way?

JONATHAN I do.

JONATHAN *leaves and* **WENDY** *follows, closing the door behind her.*

As the door closes, lights fade to blackout.

Scene change music: "A FINE ROMANCE" sung by Ella Fitzgerald and Louis Armstrong.

Duet II – Secretarial Skills

BARRIE *is dressed in colourful, quite eccentric clothes.*
JANET is in business attire. It is suggested that the
characters are American and the play set in the USA,
but this is flexible. The apartment is being decorated
for a birthday party. There is a cake box in the kitchen,
which JANET is cutting open. BARRIE is strategically
placing bottles of champagne around the room. Church
bells are heard to ring in the distance, announcing a
wedding.

BARRIE The damn bells are off again. It's the same every
Saturday. They pour in and pour out, throw around rice
and confetti and the bells ding their dong... Sometimes I
spend the whole morning watching the couples come and go.
Some of them do it with such fanfare—it's like the opening
of the Olympics. But the thing we all know is—the great
un-said on any wedding day—the horrible truth that most
of these couples will be divorced within a decade. And some
by Tuesday. Marriages never seem to last these days—that's
why people spend less on presents as each year goes by. I
mean, you can spend a fortune buying something glorious
to celebrate their marital bliss—yet you know full well that
within a few years, he'll be with someone younger, she'll be
at her mother's, and the dress will be on *Ebay*... I've come
to the conclusion that people shouldn't *give* a gift to the
happy couple, they should *rent* a gift to the happy couple.

JANET Cynic.

BARRIE I'm just being realistic. I love a good romance as much
as anyone. But the divorces keep coming at you. And that's
another thing—

JANET Are they cold?

BARRIE What?

JANET The bottles.

BARRIE Oh yes. And I've put the glasses in the freezer. Where was I?

JANET Don't ask me, I'm trying to open this box without the cake collapsing.

BARRIE Oh yes—divorce. It's all done by forms and letters, stamped and signed in legal offices. At least at the Olympics, you have an opening ceremony and a closing ceremony—so a marriage should be the same. I think that if the couple want to split, they should have to march back into the church, with the same five hundred friends and family in attendance. Return the ring and renounce the vows. Then the congregation gets to re-collect all the toasters and steak knives and *throw* them at the unhappy couple. You'd attract quite a crowd. Even *I'd* go to church for that.

The bell ringing stops.

Ah! Peace at last... Do you need a hand?

JANET No, I've got it now... Have you ever been inside?

BARRIE Inside what, dear?

JANET The church.

BARRIE Oh. No—never.

JANET It's catholic, isn't it? You could go to confession.

BARRIE Yes, I could. But I'd be there an awfully long time. I'd have to take sandwiches.

JANET They say it's a relief—confessing all your sins.

BARRIE I couldn't possibly tell him *all* my sins. The poor priest would have a heart attack. *(Looking over at the cake as it emerges from its box)* I hope the cake doesn't have one candle for each year. We'll burn the place down. *(Removing* *the cardboard and revealing a large wedding cake)* ...Janet, that's a—

JANET Wedding cake. It's all I could get at short notice. And I know how you love weddings...!

BARRIE I'm confused.

JANET You only told me you wanted a party three hours ago. This was the only large cake available without notice. Well, there was one other, but it had written all over it— "Beloved Beverly, Rest in Peace". For some reason, that one had been cancelled as well.

BARRIE Maybe Beverly changed her mind.

JANET Anyway, this one is much better for your party guests. It's very rich and completely over dressed. So it's more than appropriate.

BARRIE Oh look—it comes with people. *(Spotting the ceramic figurines that are supposed to be mounted on the top of the wedding cake—a bride and groom; picking them up)* ...Actually the groom is a bit of a looker. But she's just got the one eye and half her hand has fallen off. He must be marrying her for her money.

JANET *(heading across the room to pick up her diary)* Before I forget—remember you have a meeting Monday morning with your accountants. I've put a note under your alarm clock.

BARRIE What would I do without you?

JANET That's too scary an idea, I don't want to think about it. Anything you want to add?

BARRIE I don't think so. *(He lights up a cigarette)*

JANET I thought you decided you were cutting down.

BARRIE I did... It's not going very well. But you can pencil it in for next week.

The phone rings.

JANET *(answering the phone)* Barrie Medina's apartment. Janet speaking... Oh yes... Just a moment. *(To* BARRIE*)* It's the bed people. Can you confirm that you still want that new mattress—they have to order it.

BARRIE Yes, go ahead. I've worn the other one out.

JANET I'm not going to tell them that—you'll end up in the newspapers. *(Into the phone)* ...Yes, he'd like to go ahead and order the mattress. How long will that take to arrive? ...What? ...Six weeks?

BARRIE Six weeks! The rate I'm going I won't last the next six hours!

JANET Can you try and speed it up?

BARRIE If I die before it gets here, I'll want my deposit back.

JANET OK, thank you. Bye. *(She puts the phone down)*

BARRIE Month and a half for a mattress. Have you ever heard of such a thing?

JANET They make them by hand.

BARRIE I don't care if they make them with their *feet*! It's still far too long.

JANET Well— I think I persuaded them to speed it up.

BARRIE Thank you.

JANET ...You know what today is?

BARRIE Yes—it's my birthday.

JANET And? ...Our five-thousandth anniversary. We've been working together five-thousand days.

BARRIE Really? I should buy you a gift.

JANET You already did. I bought these shoes on your credit card.

BARRIE They're lovely—I have such good taste. Here's to the next five-thousand.

JANET If we live that long. Oh—and don't forget the Benefit next weekend.

BARRIE Benefit?

JANET For orphan children—a performance of *"Les Miserables"*.

BARRIE Oh yes, I knew it was something to do with being French and unhappy.

JANET I've got you a seat near all the celebrities.

BARRIE Anyone really famous that I can flirt with?

JANET Nicolas Cage, Matt Damon...

BARRIE Matt Damon? Ah yes—that could be very interesting...

JANET He's not gay, is he?

BARRIE Not yet, but it's a three hour show!

JANET What do you want to wear?

BARRIE Dark blue suit, bright red tie.

JANET Oh, I don't think you should wear the bright red tie—it looks like somebody cut your throat. Wouldn't the orange tie be better? Apparently orange is the new red.

BARRIE No! *Yellow* is the new red and blue is the new black. Don't you read the magazines?

JANET I don't have time!

BARRIE You make it sound like that's my fault.

JANET That's only because it is.

BARRIE Where's the show on?

JANET Theatre in the Park.

BARRIE Oh, that's handy. I can walk straight from here to there if the weather's fine.

JANET Are you sure?

BARRIE Yes. Do me good to get some fresh air. And it's a nice walk—the trees will be blossoming, the birds squawking.

JANET Squawking? It's a city park, not Jurassic Park.

BARRIE You know, last time I was there in the park—I was on my way to a conference. And I was passing by the pond, when some guy leaped out from behind a bush and flashed me!

JANET No!

BARRIE Yes, he did. Right there in full daylight.

JANET What did you do?

BARRIE Well, I made damn sure I walked home the same way! But that's not why I'm going on foot this time, before you ask.

JANET I learned not to ask five-thousand days ago. I'll cancel the car. Remember to bring your cheque book.

BARRIE Will I get a goodie bag?

JANET I believe so.

BARRIE Oh, goodie.

JANET So—shall I leave you to it?

BARRIE Aren't you staying?

JANET I think I need to just eat and get to sleep.

BARRIE Oh, nonsense. Who else is going to tuck me in tonight? Look—have a glass of champagne and a bit of cake and then later there'll be food here...won't there?

JANET Yes, we have catering. I phoned Consuelo.

BARRIE Consuelo? Oh dear—she has a face like a potato.

JANET She's a good cook, she's doing tapas. And be nice to her because she's bringing you a surprise present.

BARRIE What is it?

JANET It's a surprise!

BARRIE *waits for the answer.*

...She's knitted you a scarf.

BARRIE*'s face sinks.*

...And how thrilled she'll be to see that look of disappointment on your face.

BARRIE I don't mean to be ungrateful.

JANET Then, *don't* be.

BARRIE *lights up another cigarette.*

...Barrie!

BARRIE It's only a small one.

JANET We talked about you smoking less.

BARRIE No—*you* talked about me smoking less. I just stood there.

JANET I'm thinking of your health.

BARRIE Yes, I know, Janet, but I really do love a good cigarette.

JANET So I see. If you had your way, you'd smoke three-thousand a day. Two in your ears, two in your nose, one in your mouth and one up your—

BARRIE Janet! I'm shocked.

JANET I'll do you a deal—put it out and I'll accept that glass of champagne.

BARRIE Great! *(He stubs out the cigarette)*

JANET There's an open one in the kitchen, the cork's already loose. I may have already had one...

BARRIE *(going into the kitchen, finding the champagne, and pouring two glasses)* I'm glad you're staying. There'll be lots of single men here.

JANET I don't think those are the kind of single men I'm after.

BARRIE There will be lots for you too—divorcees, businessmen looking for love, and rich widowers. There's bound to be someone who'll catch your eye.

JANET It's too much hard work.

BARRIE But it's something you just have to do, Janet. We are all obligated to find romance. It's nature's law. *(Finishing pouring the champagne)* ...Do you want a bit of cake with this?

JANET No—don't cut into it before anybody gets here.

BARRIE *ignores her, grabs a knife and proceeds to cut out two slices of cake.*

...That's going to look very odd with chunks missing.

BARRIE It's a wedding cake. There's also a wedding missing.

JANET *collects the two glasses of champagne and* **BARRIE** *brings over the two plates of cake. They sit together on the sofa.*

Look at us—like an old married couple.

JANET Don't say things like that—you'll give me ideas...

They each take a bite of the cake.

BARRIE ...Would you like to be married?

JANET I like the idea in principle. If I can find someone remotely...you know. They say there's someone for everyone, don't they? He must be hiding. It's a pity, I'd quite like someone to adore. You'll have to do until I find him. You're pretty adorable, aren't you?

BARRIE Yes, aren't I just.

JANET I feel half married to you already. I sometimes think we should just get hitched for the hell of it. I don't see the difference. I'm here seven days a week anyway—I might as well also have the ring and the toasters.

BARRIE Now there's no need to get impatient. This is what advancing years and biology does to you—your bridal body clock is ticking. But you should enjoy the adventure more. You're single and available—love can leap out at you at any moment.

JANET From behind a bush, even.

BARRIE You're a wonderful woman. Your time will come... I promise.

JANET Don't make promises you can't keep. It may never happen. *(She downs her champagne in one large gulp)*

BARRIE *looks at her.*

...Well, you know me—glass always half empty.

BARRIE From what I see, glass *always* empty.

JANET My point is—I mean—none of us can control these things. So where's my safety net? What's my back-up plan?

BARRIE Well... I don't know. I don't have one of those either. I suppose we could knit ourselves a couple of blankets and park our wheelchairs together once a day for an ice cream.

JANET My apartment doesn't have an elevator. If I want an ice cream, I'll have to throw myself out the window. It's better that I move into this place. The elevator here is bigger than my entire room, so I could live in that. I'm quite used to all the ups and downs.

BARRIE Sorry to disappoint—but I won't be living here in my retirement. I'll use the country house.

JANET You wouldn't cope with that on your own.

BARRIE Consuelo will still be around. She'll outlive all of us. And I'll just get a housekeeper.

JANET Well, *I* could do that. I'm not going to live on my own when I'm that age. You'll have to invite me to move in with you. There'll still be paperwork to be done and I can run the house for you—and, if you behave yourself, tuck you in at night.

BARRIE Unless you're married.

JANET Well, yes... You know, about half the people I meet think we're so cosy with each other that we simply *must* be having a passionate affair.

BARRIE Don't be ridiculous.

JANET It's true. You'd be surprised.

BARRIE I would have thought it was pretty obvious that I'm—

JANET Not obvious to everyone. They see us together and figure you can draw only one possible conclusion—the wrong one.

BARRIE Well!

JANET You forget that there are a lot of people in this world for whom homosexuality simply does not exist in their own circle of friends and family. It's an impossibility. People see only what they want to see. And what they see in you is an eccentric, colourful gentleman who is *bound* to be having his wicked way with his vivacious secretary.

BARRIE I'm shocked. I shall have to take a tablet.

JANET Anyway—I accept your offer.

BARRIE You do? Good. What offer?

JANET That we'll live together—if nothing better turns up.

BARRIE Ah yes—the safety net.

JANET Precisely. So now you never need to worry about having someone to look after you... That's my birthday present to you. Cheers. *(She drains her glass)*

BARRIE I think I should have asked for a scarf.

JANET *(getting up and taking the empty glasses into the kitchen)* We need to move some of this furniture around.

BARRIE Well, hang on—if we're going to get active, I really *will* need to take a tablet.

JANET Which one? Cholesterol, diabetes, blood pressure, vitamin deficiency or gout?

BARRIE ...The *pink* one! —And don't run them off in a list like that—you make me sound dead already.

JANET I'll get it for you.

JANET *exits into the bathroom.*

BARRIE I'm not convinced about any of these tablets. I think it works against the universe's great plan—the cosmos having ordained that I should have high cholesterol and extreme blood sugar to balance out my high income and incredible dress sense... They have a pill for everything these days—except for short sightedness. Which means, of course, you can't *see* the pills you're taking for everything except short sightedness. *(He looks at himself in the mirror and pulls back the skin on his face to tighten it)*

JANET *returns with the pill in an ornate pill box.*

...I think I need plastic surgery.

JANET You're too young for that.

BARRIE Not true. Two of my friends, Michael and Tony, are only in their forties and they've already had their bags done... And next year, they're doing the ones under their eyes...! *(Looking again at his face in the mirror)* ...My face is like a very slow landslide. And a tan doesn't help. When we came back from that scorching holiday in Hawaii, I looked less like a bronzed god and more like a baked apple.

JANET *laughs.*

It's hardly funny.

JANET *(giving him the pill box)* Take your tablet. I'll get you some water. *(She proceeds to fill a glass with a bottle of Perrier water)*

BARRIE Don't you ever think about being immortal?

JANET I still don't have a clue what I'm doing on *Friday*. One step at a time.

BARRIE I should have been shot at forty.

JANET Oh, don't. It's not so bad.

BARRIE Not so bad?!

JANET Oh, the ageing process can be a bit miserable from a physical standpoint. But mentally, I really think that growing older carries great rewards. You keep with you decades of all those things you've learned. You have knowledge, wisdom. All those mistakes you'll never need to make again. And however much you get knocked back by life, you do start to appreciate the wonder of it.

BARRIE Such as?

JANET Oh, you know—nature. Leaves and trees, clouds, a dog wagging his tail. It all becomes magical. I never used to notice a thing. But now I see all the beauty in the world. Don't you?

BARRIE It's hard to see all the beauty in the world when your dentures fall into your cornflakes.

JANET bursts out laughing.

It's not funny, Janet. It's a very depressing sight, seeing them floating there in the semi-skimmed. It makes me extremely miserable despite the fact it makes my dentist extremely happy. His eyes light up in dollar signs whenever I walk in the clinic. I open my mouth and he starts designing his new jacuzzi. But his joy is my tragedy. So never mind trees and flowers—I'm growing old!

JANET Your dentures are hardly the result of advancing years—I'm quite certain the seven tons of toffee you eat every day doesn't help either.

BARRIE Oh don't mention the toffee! Now I have to have some.

JANET Absolutely not. You've got all that cake to get through. Take your pill.

BARRIE *(struggling to get the pill out of the box)* I can't even get to the damn thing. This box is extremely pretty but totally useless...like most of the men I know. *(He gets the pill from the box and pops it in his mouth)*

JANET *gives him the glass of water.*

(swallowing the pill) ...You really do look after me. Maybe I *should* marry you.

JANET Maybe I should accept! Marrying a gay man is far from the craziest thing a woman can do in this chaotic world.

BARRIE But, as ideas go, it's not exactly romantic.

JANET And you think *straight* men are romantic? I know women who go out and buy *themselves* a valentine's card. Then take it home and ask their husbands if they wouldn't mind signing it! One woman I know even gets a stamp and puts it in the post! Plus, every wife needs to remind her man of the date of St. Valentine's *and* of their wedding anniversary and, if they get really lucky, the constant reminders and subtle hints might result in a cheap box of chocolates from the petrol station... And the husband will then eat most of them! Romance rarely comes included in the package. The best you can hope for is friendship and companionship and someone like *you* could provide that as well as any eligible bachelor.

BARRIE That doesn't mean it's the *right* thing. Oh—for bugger's sake, we couldn't get married even if we were serious. Imagine the fight over who gets to wear the dress!

JANET *(laughing at this)* Well, even so, we wouldn't be the first.

BARRIE Oh, that's true enough...but I would like to see you with a husband. A real husband, I mean. And if you did have a wedding, I'd *rent* you a beautiful gift.

JANET Save your money. I'm never going to find him. I think my standards are too high. It's just so very difficult to find someone *nice* who's not already been snapped up. What would you do, if you were in my shoes?

BARRIE I'd get a purse to match.

JANET Stop joking! I'm serious.

BARRIE You just need to open your eyes. Wander about, take a look around—see what catches your attention.

JANET But I *hate* window shopping. Oh, Barrie. If only you were...

BARRIE Well, thank God I'm not. You wouldn't be able to keep your hands off.

JANET Women don't always crave sex you know. Sometimes we're only looking for affection and companionship. That's what we *really* want—not a ten minute roll in the hay. Men don't seem to realise that gentle words and an act of kindness can be very sexual—and often perfectly sufficient. Unless of course you're irresistible...which you're not—not quite. Come on, let's move the sofa.

They proceed to pick the sofa up and carry it across the room. When half way across the room with it, JANET asks a question.

...Do you like being gay?

BARRIE (*nearly dropping the sofa on hearing this*) What?!

JANET Well, it's not a ridiculous question, is it?

BARRIE Not the way today is going— No, I suppose it isn't.

JANET So? I'm interested.

They put the sofa down in its new position.

BARRIE OK—you want a serious answer?

JANET That would make a nice change.

BARRIE The answer is *yes*, I like it very much.

JANET Really? Why?

BARRIE *Why*? Well—aside from the fact I've no choice in the matter—I guess I've just always rather liked the way it marks you out from the start as being different—regardless of whether you originally wanted to be or not. It forces you to have a different outlook on the world, to be a little apart from everybody else's headlong rush into normality. It sets you on a different path—and that feels good...most of the time... I suppose I just like living outside of the general rules—for people not to have the same expectations of me. I'm *unexpected.* And that's delightful. I honestly feel that being "the same" would be very dull.

JANET *(thinking for a moment)* ...Kiss me.

BARRIE *(shocked)* ...Excuse me?

JANET Just—kiss me.

BARRIE I don't know where on earth your head is today—it must be the—

> **JANET** *suddenly reaches forward, clasps* **BARRIE***'s head in her hands, and kisses him passionately on the lips. After a prolonged locking of lips, she withdraws and looks into his eyes for a reaction.*

—Those are fabulous ear-rings. *(Examining* **JANET***'s ear-rings more closely)* ...Did *I* buy those?

JANET ...Didn't you feel *anything*?

BARRIE It was—not unpleasant.

JANET "Not unpleasant"? Well—I guess that settles it.

BARRIE Settles what?

JANET *(setting about moving the chairs around the room; changing the subject)* What about the chairs—where are we going to put those?

BARRIE Sod the *chairs*! Janet, I'm sorry to interrupt your nervous breakdown, but—I think perhaps we ought to talk about this.

JANET No, that's all right. *(She starts moving the chairs around)*

BARRIE *(watching her, bemused at first and then a moment of realisation)* ...I know what this is. And it's all my fault. I've dominated all your time, made you endlessly rush around for me, and in the process I've stolen your entire social life from you and stripped away all opportunity for partnership. I'm so sorry. You need a life beyond these four walls so you can have time to flirt with men. Any men. You need to get out there and flirt them within an inch of their lives.

JANET But maybe I don't need a man. So long as I have you to look after.

BARRIE That's not enough! No—I'm not letting you give up that easily. I'm making sure you walk down that aisle.

JANET If I get any fatter, I'll *be* the aisle.

BARRIE *(physically stopping **JANET** manoeuvring the chairs and making her listen to him)* You, Janet, are a beautiful, beautiful woman.

JANET Only two "beautiful"s? I must be losing my touch.

BARRIE You are an attractive, intelligent and—occasionally very scary—woman. You're a catch.

JANET He'll need a damn big net.

BARRIE Any man would be *lucky* to have you. Even I, with my unique ability to see the *worst* in everyone, have nothing but love for you. You are lovable—and I love you—though I'm sorry that I can't...*love* you. But I can at least clearly see your virtues from where I stand in the world. And surely all those men out there will be able to see them too. But—you need to be on display! You need to show yourself.

JANET I don't have the energy. *(She sits down on the chair she was carrying)*

BARRIE ...I'll tell you something—my parents broke up when I was a young man. On the day the divorce was finalised, my father was sitting alone at home in front of the TV and he suddenly said to himself, "Right—that's it". He got in the car, drove to the nearest singles bar and, in the following hours, found himself a new lady friend. A week later, she moved in with him. And they stayed together until the day he died.

JANET But was he happy?

BARRIE Yes. Yes, he was. Because to have a female companion, whoever she was, was enough for him. It wasn't about perfect matches or high and low standards. He knew what he needed to live a contented life—just to be with *someone*—and so he went out and found that for himself. That's what it's all about. Not the expectations of society or family—but working out what you *need*... What do you need?

JANET I think I need a drink.

BARRIE ...And I think you need a fresh start.

JANET So, how do I—

BARRIE I've got it! —I'm sending you on a cruise!

JANET *(getting up from her chair)* What?! I don't want a—

BARRIE No arguments. Not a word. You know you mustn't disagree with me. The doctor says it raises my cholesterol.

JANET But Barrie—

BARRIE I hear a cruise is incredibly pleasant. You get to see different cities, catch some sun. There's a full programme of sports—and they feed you twenty-five times a day. Which of course means you can't play any of the sports. But nonetheless it's an adventure and the dinners are fantastic.

JANET I hate eating alone.

BARRIE No—not alone. They sit you at huge tables with complete strangers.

JANET Who might be horrible.

BARRIE It's possible, yes, but—

JANET Barrie—if I want to have a meal with people I don't know or like, I can visit my family!

BARRIE But you're missing the point. This would be a "singles" cruise. Almost everyone would be available.

JANET And a sad old bastard.

BARRIE Don't knock "sad old bastards". I've had some very happy weekends with "sad old bastards". It's precisely what you need—it's perfect for you! And if you don't like the passengers, you can try your chances with the entertainment crew—or one of the actors.

JANET Actors! You want me to go out with an actor!

BARRIE Oh, actors are fine, very easy to please. Whenever they do anything, you just give them a round of applause.

JANET Even in bed?

BARRIE Depends on how many encores you want... Yes, yes—this is a great idea. I'm paying for everything and I'm booking it tomorrow.

JANET But—

BARRIE I won't hear another word against it. *(Going to the door and throwing it open)* So get home and pack for the high seas.

JANET My God, you really are serious.

BARRIE Yes—absolutely.

JANET Well... *(Walking up to him)* ...then why don't you come with me?

BARRIE But that would completely defeat the—

JANET No. I'd still be on parade. It's just that—I'd have a fall-back position. If things didn't go as planned, I'd have a friend there, a companion... You do need a bit of sun.

BARRIE ...You think?

JANET Oh yes. *(Closing the door)* You've been looking very pale recently.

BARRIE I should take a tablet.

JANET It's your *birthday*. You should take a *cruise*.

BARRIE *(considering the suggestion)* ...Oh, go on, then—yes I'll go with you!

JANET *(delighted and jumping with joy)* Oh yes!! Oh—we'll have such fun. I'll get straight on the internet and book something.

BARRIE Wait! What about the party?

JANET Oh yes. Well, first thing tomorrow, then. I'll sort out *everything*.

BARRIE I'm excited.

JANET Me too.

BARRIE We're going on a cruise!

They give each other an excited hug.

...Though I still think my presence is bound to stop you husband shopping.

JANET I don't need a sad old bastard—I already have you! Extremely rich and no interest in having sex—the perfect travelling companion. I wouldn't dream of sailing into the sunset with anybody else.

BARRIE Well, you can't argue with good taste.

They hug again. The church bells begin to chime again.

JANET Now let's get this cake sorted into portions. The quicker they eat, the quicker they leave, and the sooner we can book the holiday. *(She dashes into the kitchen and grabs a big cake knife)*

The two of them then go over to the cake and, both holding the knife, make the first cut. As they do so, the wedding bells continue to chime, capturing them in a typical bride and groom image.

BARRIE *(thinking for a moment)* Janet—did I happen to mention in our conversation—

JANET Hm?

BARRIE ...Did I tell you that I loved you?

JANET Yes, several times.

BARRIE Good... Good...

They give each other a quick peck of a kiss.

Blackout.

End of Act I

ACT II

Duet III – The Holiday

The characters are on holiday in Spain and wear typical colourful attire for a beach vacation. The apartment is decorated to resemble a Spanish villa. There is a brightly coloured throw on the settee. The door opens. From outside, we hear Spanish pop music and the sounds of a party complete with flashing lights, etc. The song heard playing at the party is— "NOBODY WANTS TO BE LONELY" sung by Ricky Martin and Christina Aguilera.

BOBBY *enters, a little tipsy and carrying a large cocktail complete with umbrella, etc.*

BOBBY Shelley? Shelley!

SHELLEY *emerges from behind the kitchen wall. She is wearing a sombrero and is also carrying an extravagant cocktail. She is quite drunk.*

SHELLEY I'm here! I'm looking for a *cerveza.*

BOBBY What about your cocktail?

SHELLEY I'm thinking beyond the cocktail. *After* the cocktail, I want a *cerveza.*

BOBBY For goodness sake—just drink the cocktail and worry about the beer later. You always get ahead of yourself.

SHELLEY That's how you progress in life. *Don't* live for this moment—use it to plan the next one.

BOBBY You're drunk.

SHELLEY This isn't drunk! *(Tossing her sombrero aside)* You should know what I'm like when I'm *really* drunk.

BOBBY Yeah, I already got the T-shirt. Are you going back to the party?

SHELLEY It's not a party—it's a *fiesta*.

BOBBY Are you?

SHELLEY No. The tanned dark Spanish men are all chatting me up. It's unbearable!

BOBBY Then maybe you shouldn't chat back.

SHELLEY It's harmless fun. I'm completely in control. *(She drinks her entire cocktail in one go)*

BOBBY Shelley! You didn't even taste it!

SHELLEY Calm down. It's non-alcoholic.

BOBBY No, it isn't. *(Showing his drink) This* is the non-alcoholic one.

SHELLEY Oh... Then give it to me. *(Taking* **BOBBY***'s cocktail and starting to consume it)* It'll cancel the other one out.

BOBBY It doesn't actually work like that. We should probably eat something, soak up all the drink.

SHELLEY But you're not drunk.

BOBBY No—but perhaps a little tipsy. Everything in moderation.

SHELLEY That's right. How very, very careful of you.

BOBBY One doesn't want to make a fool of oneself, does one?

SHELLEY Stop it—too many numbers.

BOBBY *(taking the cocktail from* **SHELLEY** *and putting it to one side)* What do you want to eat?

SHELLEY ...*Paella*!

BOBBY There might be some crisps.

SHELLEY Crisps? I'm in *España*, I don't want crisps. I want *chorizo* and *Serrano* ham.

BOBBY *(locating a packet of digestive biscuits)* Ah—biscuits!

SHELLEY What are *they* doing here?

BOBBY I brought them for the journey.

SHELLEY You brought biscuits? You xenophobic heathen.

BOBBY You packed tea bags!

SHELLEY That's different! They can't make proper tea here. It's a sea of *espresso*.

BOBBY *(offering* **SHELLEY** *a biscuit)* Just have one.

SHELLEY No. It's pathetic and boring to bring your own biscuits on holiday. I refuse! *(Thinking for a second and then taking a biscuit; throwing herself on the sofa)* ...Have you got an aspirin?

BOBBY Do you have a headache?

SHELLEY I'm planning ahead.

A knock on the door. **BOBBY** *goes to answer it. As he opens the door, we again experience the noise, music and lights beyond.*

BOBBY *(speaking to a person beyond the door)* Hola! Oh—for Shelley? ...Yes, I'll give it to her... Yes. *Ole!* *(He closes the door. He holds in his hand a business card which has just been given to him)* ...This is for you, apparently.

SHELLEY *(not looking)* Is it drinkable?

BOBBY No, it's a chiropractor. *(Reading the card)* "Carlos Gonzalez" —ring any bells?

SHELLEY *(looking over at him)* Oh—wasn't he the tall one?

BOBBY How should I know.

SHELLEY I expect he's looking for romance.

BOBBY No. The way your back creaks every time you bend over, I expect he's looking for a patient. Or perhaps they want to make a study of how it is you're still standing after so many cocktails. Did you know that when you get drunk, you often stand at a thirty-three degree angle? It's a miracle of science you don't fall over. You're like the leaning tower of Pisa. *(He crosses and gives her the business card)*

SHELLEY *(holding it precariously)* I'll take that beer now.

BOBBY No, you won't.

SHELLEY Excuse me, Bobby—but you have no domain over me.

BOBBY And what a relief that is. *(He eats another biscuit)*

SHELLEY Oh those bloody biscuits! Each crunch cuts through me like a rusty sword. Put them away!

> **BOBBY** *turns to head back to the kitchen.*

Wait!

> **BOBBY** *pauses and* **SHELLEY** *takes another biscuit.* **BOBBY** *then heads into the kitchen.*

SHELLEY *(eating)* ...What else have we got?

BOBBY Just the *papas fritas* and a jar of olives.

SHELLEY Good! We can have a picnic. *(She gets up from the sofa. She removes the throw and lays it out on the floor like a regular rug, then she takes off her shoes and sits on the rug)* ...See—isn't this great? An indoor picnic! No driving, no grass, no flies. Outdoor picnics are stupid. No ants here.

BOBBY No food either. *(He brings over the crisps and olives and places them on the rug)*

SHELLEY Would you care to join me?

BOBBY Isn't it, perhaps, time for bed?

SHELLEY No—that'll be when "Carlos" gets here.

BOBBY Carlos has no interest in romance. He just wants to do a quick spinal adjustment.

SHELLEY Oh, is that what they're calling it these days? You're just jealous of the attention I'm getting.

BOBBY Not anymore... *(He eats some crisps)*

SHELLEY *(eating an olive)* ...Are you glad we came?

BOBBY Well, we both needed a bit of sun.

SHELLEY You can get sun anywhere.

BOBBY Yes, but this bit of sun was already paid for.

SHELLEY I think everyone at home thought it a bit strange.

BOBBY It would have been stupid just to throw it away. Neither of us can afford to be so casual with our finances. Anyway, like I say—it's been good to be warm for a few days. And I'd rather deal with everything here in the sunshine. Doing it at home engulfed in clouds and rain would be far too grey an experience. One should never get *divorced* in bad weather.

SHELLEY Don't say that word, I don't like hearing it.

BOBBY I can't help what it's called.

SHELLEY All the same...

There is another knock on the door.

BOBBY Who is it this time—your orthodontist?

SHELLEY Oh, don't answer it. I'm off men. From now on, my only passion is food. Whenever I have sexual cravings, I'm going to avoid male company and put a nice dish in the oven.

BOBBY Have you considered lesbianism?

SHELLEY I was thinking more of a shepherd's pie...!

Another knock on the door.

...How do you say "get lost" in Spanish? They're not coming in—I'm not sharing my lovely picnic.

BOBBY You know... I wouldn't mind if you found someone else—Latino or otherwise. Not tonight, I mean, but generally—in the future. I wouldn't mind if you found—someone new...

SHELLEY Really? Don't you want me to grow old and alone?

BOBBY At first, I did. But one has to be mature about these things.

SHELLEY And we are being bizarrely mature, aren't we? Most divorcing couples get lawyers. We get drunk in Torremolinos.

BOBBY I'm not drunk. I'm just squiffy.

SHELLEY Squiffy or not, we're either incredibly sensible or unbelievably stupid. I still can't quite believe we got on the plane.

BOBBY It was already paid for—no refunds.

SHELLEY Yes, but sometimes you just have to cut your losses. Circumstances change and—well...it's no longer appropriate.

BOBBY You didn't have to come. I would have been perfectly happy here on my own.

SHELLEY But half of this holiday is mine. And we agreed that we'd each get half of everything. I wanted to make that point sincsuccly—

BOBBY Succinctly!

SHELLEY Half of everything. Including half of this half-arsed holiday.

BOBBY I have never disagreed with that arrangement... The only exception, of course, being the limited editions.

SHELLEY Excuse me?

BOBBY Well—they're mine, aren't they? The giclée prints and the car models—they're mine.

SHELLEY Not so fast, Long John Silver. Is that what this picnic is all about? Get me relaxed and drunk so you can—

BOBBY I didn't get you drunk. *You* got you drunk. I was the other side of the room while you were scuba diving in a vat of piña coladas.

SHELLEY Half of those prints and models are mine.

BOBBY You don't even know what half of them are. You don't *want* them.

SHELLEY I *do* want them. Especially the—red car thing.

BOBBY It's a model of a Ferrari.

SHELLEY Yes, I know it is. And I want it. I want the Fenarri.

BOBBY *(correcting her)* Ferrari.

SHELLEY Look—I'm only asking for what I'm entitled to. Half!

BOBBY ...All right then. I'll take half the fish.

SHELLEY You hate the fish.

BOBBY I'll learn to love them. I'll have the boxy yellow one and the red spiky thing.

SHELLEY *(horrified he doesn't know their names)* Harrison and Brad!

BOBBY Yes, those two. I'll have them with chips! *(He gets up and strides off)*

SHELLEY *(getting up also; carrying the jar of olives with her)* You're not playing fair.

BOBBY It's not a game, Shelley. It's the end of a marriage.

SHELLEY We wouldn't be in this situation at all if you hadn't had five affairs!

BOBBY I did not have five affairs. I had five nights with the same woman.

SHELLEY It's the same thing! *(She throws an olive into her mouth)*

BOBBY And what about you and Thomas? I suppose that doesn't count?

SHELLEY He was my school sweetheart. It wasn't a *new* thing. I was re-kindling an *old* thing. Didn't you know "Retro" was back in fashion?

Another knock on the door. **SHELLEY** *goes to answer it. She opens the door to be greeted by the usual music, noise and lights. She appears to be being offered something.*

Oh... OK, then. *Gracias. (She is handed another huge cocktail. Accepting it, she gives over the jar of olives in exchange, though she's not sure why. She shuts the door)*

BOBBY Haven't you had enough?

SHELLEY Of the cocktails, no. Of you, yes.

BOBBY Then that's perfect. We fly home Saturday and you never have to see me again.

SHELLEY Oh, stop it. We can't get rid of each other that easy. First we have to sort out who gets what.

BOBBY We've covered all that. There were just those few other tiny things to deal with—and I thought—

SHELLEY You thought you'd keep all if it.

BOBBY No—just the things that were personal to me. And why would you want those?

SHELLEY Precisely for that reason. I want something that was personal to you. I am not one of those people who wants to wipe the board clean as though this marriage never happened. I want to keep hold of a little bit of everything we shared together. I want a little bit of you.

BOBBY Why?

SHELLEY Because it's too many years to let go of. Now give me the damn Farore.

BOBBY It's Ferrari! Farore was the Greek goddess of courage.

SHELLEY Well, now we know who got the encyclopedias!

BOBBY You should read more. It might do you good.

SHELLEY I don't need to read. I have other areas of expertise.

BOBBY Such as?

SHELLEY *(taking a gulp of her drink and swishing it round her mouth before swallowing)* One shot rum, one shot Malibu, a dash of cassis, lemonade and a spoonful of grenadine. *(Slamming the drink down on a nearby surface)* ...Now stick that up your Acropolis.

BOBBY I'm going to pack.

SHELLEY Pack?!

BOBBY Yes. I'm catching an earlier flight home and hiring a lawyer.

SHELLEY Oh, well that's very timid of you. I wonder what the Greek goddess of courage would have to say about that.

BOBBY *storms into the bedroom.*

...Fine! I'm going back to the party. *(She heads for the door)*

BOBBY *emerges from the bedroom with his suitcase in one hand and a pile of clothes in the other. He opens the case and throws the clothes into it.*

There's no point packing now. There are no planes at three in the morning.

BOBBY *(sarcastically)* Then I'll take a train.

SHELLEY There are no trains across the ocean, you idiot.

BOBBY I meant the train to Madrid and then a flight from there. Double idiot!

SHELLEY So you're walking out on me—again!

BOBBY No, I'm just cutting short a holiday. Because it was a stupid, stupid idea.

SHELLEY Oh stop overreacting.

BOBBY We agreed we'd make this civilised.

SHELLEY I *was* being civilised. You were the one that lost your rag.

BOBBY *carries on packing his suitcase.*

...That's the thing about men—it's all head of the household, hunter and gatherer, but underneath you're still in short trousers. All we have to do is snap at you and you jump like frightened rabbits.

BOBBY Don't talk rubbish. *(He grabs the packet of biscuits)*

SHELLEY *(snapping)* Not the biscuits!!

BOBBY *lurches away from the biscuits like a frightened rabbit. He then diverts his attention to his spare pair of shoes, as* **SHELLEY** *takes another drink from her cocktail.* **BOBBY** *throws the shoes into the case.*

...Oh, look—you can't just throw things on top of each other like that. The shoes will get ruined and your shirts will—just let me do it.

She goes over to him and hands him the cocktail. She then gets down on her knees and starts to reorganise the case. **BOBBY** *lets her go ahead, sipping her drink.*

Another knock on the door. **BOBBY** *goes to answer it. He opens the door to the noise, music and lights. He is being offered something, so he reaches out to collect it. It is the empty olive jar. Confused by what is happening, he hands over the cocktail. The door closes.*

BOBBY *(standing there holding the empty jar; bemused)* I'm not quite sure what happened there...

SHELLEY *(looking over at him)* Hey! Where's my drink?

BOBBY Don't start on me—I panicked. I gave it back to them.

SHELLEY Why?

BOBBY I said—I don't know. But we got the jar back... Oh don't say it—I'm a hopeless fool, right? *(Sarcastic)* No wonder you married me.

SHELLEY That's exactly right. I was always weak at the knees when some hopeless fool was around me. It's my mothering instinct. You met my ex, didn't you? And the guy I dated at college—remember what they were like?

BOBBY ...Hopeless fools.

SHELLEY Precisely. Though—and this is a compliment—you turned out to be less hopeless and less of a fool than I originally thought.

BOBBY Sorry to have disappointed you.

SHELLEY Oh, you didn't disappoint me... Now where are your pyjamas?

BOBBY Under the pillow.

SHELLEY *goes into the bedroom.*

(putting the jar down) ...And don't forget my slippers!

The pair of Mickey Mouse slippers come flying across the room at him.

...Yep, those are the ones.

SHELLEY *returns, carrying his pyjamas, which she drops into the case.*

BOBBY *picks up the slippers.*

SHELLEY There, that's most of your clothes. The rest I'll drop off on Saturday. Pop those in here.

He puts the slippers in the case.

So now you just need your passport, your wallet and book seven of Harry Potter—then you're ready to go. *(She closes the case shut)* Oh—and by the way—those Harry Potter books are for *children*. I've been meaning to mention it the last eight years.

BOBBY It's an *adult* edition.

SHELLEY It's the *same* book with a plainer cover. Didn't they tell you that at *Toys R Us*?

BOBBY Just leave *Harry* out of this.

SHELLEY *(carrying the case to the middle of the room and planting it there)* There. Bon voyage! Away you go! Goodbye! Adios!

BOBBY Adi-bloody-os!

BOBBY *leaves with his case in hand.*

SHELLEY *closes the door. She stands alone in the room for a moment. She checks her watch. Then opens the door again.*

As expected, **BOBBY** *is standing right outside, case still in hand. He walks back into the room.*

BOBBY Where am I supposed to get a taxi at this time of night. That lot opposite will be hiring everything on wheels. I'll go when I'm good and ready—in an hour or two. *(Putting the case down)* ...Or wait till the morning.

SHELLEY Or even...

BOBBY ...Or hold off till Saturday. *(Looking at her)* You don't know me as well as you think you do.

SHELLEY I shall miss these little pocket dramas when you've gone.

BOBBY I was just making a point. *(He goes and sits on the rug on the floor and eats a biscuit)*

SHELLEY ...And to think I had such high hopes for this divorce. A slap on the back and a gentlemanly shaking of hands. A quick sharing of the spoils, a kiss on the cheek, and then away we go—you in the Fiat, me in the Toyota. On paper, it would have looked so easy.

BOBBY Actually I wanted to talk to you about the Toyota...

SHELLEY Oh, have the bloody Toyota! And the bloody models. Just give me one thing, would you, just one thing.

BOBBY *looks at her.*

...That picture of the couple sat on the beach together. I like that painting. It reminds me of our honeymoon.

BOBBY We went to London. There's no beach in London.

SHELLEY The figures, I mean, the image of it. Two lost souls just sitting there—holding hands.

BOBBY Is that how you saw us?

SHELLEY That's how we were. You've forgotten already.

BOBBY I'm sorry it didn't work out.

SHELLEY ...Me too. But just know that I have no regrets—I'm glad I married you. There—I said it. Now you can sod off without feeling guilty... And, hey, who knows—maybe we can just become good friends.

BOBBY *laughs at this suggestion.*

...I know. It sounded stupid when I said it.

He holds up a biscuit as a peace treaty. She accepts it and sits next to him on the rug.

BOBBY It's going to be odd being single again.

SHELLEY It's not an ending—it's a beginning.

He stares at her.

...I read it in a book somewhere. We should find the author and throw it at him.

BOBBY *smiles at her and she smiles back. He offers out his hand and she holds it. They sit on the rug for a moment, just looking ahead and holding hands.*

...Are we going back to the party?

BOBBY It's not a party, it's a *fiesta*.

SHELLEY Are we?

BOBBY No, I think I'll stay here. I'm tired. I might go to bed and read.

SHELLEY Snuggle down with the hobbits.

BOBBY Not hobbits—wizards.

SHELLEY Ah yes—wizards...! *(Letting go of his hand)* Shall I unpack your pyjamas?

BOBBY No. I thought I'd sleep without them tonight. Your last chance to see me naked. Think of it as a farewell gift.

SHELLEY I'd have preferred a fruit basket...!

BOBBY *(getting up)* ...You can go back to the party, if you want. I don't mind. It's the last bit of the holiday, you shouldn't waste the opportunity to let your hair down.

SHELLEY Well, there was one other cocktail I wanted to try.

BOBBY There you go. You do that. I'll see you in the morning... Goodnight, ex-wife.

SHELLEY Goodnight, ex-husband.

BOBBY *goes into the bedroom.*

SHELLEY *watches him go. She draws a large breath and lets it out. Then she gets up and finds her bottle of perfume. Two sprays on her neck and an extra one down her chest. She then tidies herself quickly, goes to the door, and opens it.*

The music, noise and lights hit her. She pauses for a moment, thinking things over. She decides to stay in the room. She closes the door. Silence. She turns around and looks across to the bedroom.

After a few seconds, the bedroom door opens again and **BOBBY** *enters the room.*

Not noticing **SHELLEY** *at first,* **BOBBY** *goes to a corner of the room to collect his Harry Potter book. He notices* **SHELLEY** *as he is about to return to the bedroom with his book. He looks at her.*

Fancy having an extra marital affair...?

BOBBY What?

SHELLEY I don't want to end up in the sack with some Spaniard. They're all passion and fireworks. I don't like fireworks. It's just a lot of banging and always over far too quickly.

BOBBY I'm sure if we had lawyers, they'd very strongly advise against it.

SHELLEY Well, it's a good job we don't have lawyers then, isn't it?

BOBBY It won't make breaking up easier. In fact I'm sure it—

SHELLEY I just... I just don't want it to end in chaos. I want it to end...*gently.* Don't people ever split up gently?

BOBBY I don't think so.

SHELLEY Then perhaps we could start a trend... Oh, come on, Bobby. I'm not suggesting anything intimate. Just sex.

BOBBY I'm not sure.

SHELLEY Well...in this situation...what would Harry do?

BOBBY ...Oh, sod Harry! *(He energetically tosses the Harry Potter book away)*

They smile at each other. **SHELLEY** *then walks towards* **BOBBY**. *But when she gets close, she stops, full of sudden doubt, and puts her face in her hands.*

SHELLEY Oh God—what are we doing?

BOBBY *(taking* **SHELLEY**'s *hands and moving them away from her face)* We're just saying goodbye. *(He holds her hands and leads her into the bedroom)*

SHELLEY Gently...?

BOBBY Gently...

They disappear into the bedroom.

Fade to blackout.

Scene change music: **"ME AND MY SHADOW"** *sung by Robbie Williams and Jonathan Wilkes.*

As the set and props are prepared for the next play, we watch silhouettes of the actors quickly changing costume, hair, etc. Lights should rise on the next play as the song ends.

Duet IV – The Bride-To-Be

TOBY *is dressed in a dark suit.* **ANGELA** *wears a wedding dress and flowers in her hair. Both characters are suggested to be upper/middle class and British, but this is flexible. The apartment is filled with bunches of flowers and wrapped gifts.*

TOBY *enters. He casts his eye over the various flower arrangements disapprovingly. He checks his watch. He sits in a chair upstage centre and checks his mobile phone for messages.* **ANGELA** *enters from the bedroom. She is wearing a huge, flowing off-white/vanilla wedding dress.* **TOBY** *sees her and stands up, leaving his mobile on the chair.*

TOBY Angela—look at you. All of you. Is that designed for just the one person?

ANGELA No—I also have the bridesmaids under here. What do you think?

TOBY You look lovely.

ANGELA Thank you. I wish I could return the compliment.

TOBY This is my favourite suit.

ANGELA It's your only suit. You had it on for Jenny's christening, Dad's funeral, Uncle John's memorial and, I believe, it made an appearance at the opening night of *"Oklahoma"*.

TOBY Actually it was *"Cats"*.

ANGELA Nobody wears a suit to see *"Cats"*.

TOBY It was wash day.

ANGELA You could have splashed out on something new. It *is* my wedding.

TOBY Oh, is that what it is? I wondered what all the fuss was about.

Well, at least I came.

ANGELA What do you mean?

TOBY I thought I might skip this one and wait for the next.

ANGELA This is only the third occasion, Toby, it is not something I'm making a habit of... How does everything look?

TOBY Downstairs? Well—fine. Almost lavish.

ANGELA Did the flowers arrive? All the flowers?

TOBY There's certainly a representation of flowers. In very strange exotic mixes. Everything clashes. I can only presume the displays were put together by a colour-blind Mexican.

ANGELA But there *are* flowers?

TOBY There are.

ANGELA Then just say "yes". Everything doesn't need a critique. If I want an opinion on something, I shall ask for it.

TOBY But you so rarely do ask for it.

ANGELA Only because you have such bloody good taste—and I'd rather not be told when something at my wedding is horrid. You'll note I have avoided too many questions about your opinion of my dress.

TOBY Yes, that was noted.

ANGELA You don't like it?

TOBY I have no opinion.

ANGELA What's wrong with it?

TOBY I didn't say anything was wrong with it.

ANGELA Yes, you did. Your silence was deafening.

TOBY It's fine.

ANGELA Fine?! Right—that's it, I'm jumping off a tall building.

TOBY Well, you already have the parachute.

ANGELA Toby!

TOBY I'm joking, I'm joking. He's not marrying you for the dress, don't worry about it. After today you'll never see it again. Unless, of course—

ANGELA No, there will *not* be another wedding after this. This is my last marriage. It will absolutely be "until death us do part" —even if that means I have to kill him.

TOBY That's the spirit.

ANGELA *(spinning around in the dress, showing it off)* So—just tell me it's not terrible.

TOBY It's not terrible. Really. And it will look lovely in the sunshine.

ANGELA We've missed the sunshine. It clouded over the moment his mother arrived.

TOBY Well, that's fine too. It'll look less white and more vanilla.

ANGELA It's not vanilla, it's antique white or egg shell.

TOBY Not meringue?

ANGELA No, because if they called it meringue, that would imply the bride is going to look fat in it. And the bride refuses to be preoccupied by her weight, because the bride has become at peace with her waist and hips. Three months of rice crackers and vegetable soup and still I look like puff pastry. So I don't care anymore. Keeping trim is a constant battle.

TOBY You might win the battle, but you'll never win the war.

ANGELA How long have we got?

TOBY A few minutes. Number Three is already outside in the car.

ANGELA Don't call him Number Three—his name is Simon.

TOBY Ah, yes.

ANGELA You are going to be nice to him, aren't you?

TOBY I'm nice to everybody.

ANGELA That would be lovely, if it was true. You always put your foot in it and upset everybody.

TOBY I don't mean to insult. I just make passing comment.

ANGELA You told Aunty Babs she looked like a sofa!

TOBY That wasn't being nasty, that was being precise. A big flowery dress with padded shoulders and trims everywhere. I didn't know whether to bring her a drink or cover her with scatter cushions.

ANGELA She never recovered from you saying that. The dress went straight back to the shop. Is she here? *(She goes into the kitchen where she wets a tissue and, during the following dialogue, uses it to neaten her lipstick)*

TOBY I don't know, I've been up here most of the time looking after you.

ANGELA I don't need looking after. I'm not your baby sister anymore.

TOBY Sorry to disappoint you, but you'll always be my baby sister.

ANGELA *(spotting the coffee jug)* Pour me a coffee, would you?

TOBY A coffee?

ANGELA It'll give me a bit of a kick, keep me wide awake for everything. I don't want to go through the wedding half asleep.

TOBY Why not? You went through your last marriage half asleep.

ANGELA I knew you didn't like him.

TOBY I did like him. But one day he left you—and then I *didn't* like him.

ANGELA From what I saw, you never got on. Not from day one.

TOBY Actually that isn't true. Can I get a drink?

ANGELA I'd order you a coffee, but the service is quite slow.

TOBY I had something stronger in mind. Whisky?

ANGELA Now?

TOBY It's the latest thing for weight loss. The Drinking Man's Diet. You have at least twelve alcoholic drinks a day and then eat whatever you want.

ANGELA Does it work?

TOBY No—but you have a *marvellous* time!

ANGELA gets a bottle of whisky from the kitchen cupboard and gives it to TOBY along with a glass.

Any ice?

ANGELA Don't push your luck. Now are you going to get me that coffee?

TOBY It's right there next to you.

ANGELA I don't want to spill it. And so?

TOBY *(pouring himself a drink)* What?

ANGELA Do you agree that you didn't get on with him?

TOBY With who?

ANGELA Number Two! There—you see, now you've got me at it. Paul. We were talking about Paul.

TOBY Does it really matter anymore?

ANGELA Yes. Today is my day for closure. To shut one door as another opens.

TOBY Well... *(Taking a drink)* I thought he was just fine until the day I brought Kristina over to meet him. I don't think he'd ever met a feminist before and seemed quite shocked that she didn't desire to spend the entire day in the kitchen stuffing mushrooms. Each time she shared her outlook on the role of women in society, his face looked confused as to whether it should laugh, cry or explode. And when I announced that the thing that really attracted me to her was precisely her strong feminist views, I feared he might die of shock. At which point, I questioned why my sister had married this man whose moral outlook on life was trapped in nineteen-fifty six. Which, presumably, was when he bought those cardigans.

ANGELA I liked his cardigans.

TOBY Love is blind. As, I gather, was his tailor.

ANGELA And Simon? What do you think of my fiancé's wardrobe? Very sporty.

TOBY Yes. I like sporty. Though I wouldn't have necessarily worn trainers to walk my bride down the aisle.

ANGELA They're not trainers, they're sports shoes. He finds regular shoes uncomfortable, always has. They squeeze his feet.

TOBY Isn't that your job?

ANGELA You do like him, don't you?

TOBY What is it with all these questions? You've been ignoring my opinion on everything for years.

ANGELA But today I'm asking for it. Tell me.

TOBY Stop being ridiculous. It doesn't matter.

ANGELA Of course it matters—I'm about to marry him.

TOBY Yes, but presumably you made your own mind up about that. Why should you give a damn what anybody else thinks?

ANGELA I just—I would just like confirmation that I'm doing the right thing.

TOBY *(gesturing to her wedding dress)* It's a little late for that! We have no time for last minute nerves. There are over a hundred people in the garden next door awaiting us. Dark clouds hover overhead and the ants are eating their way through the buffet. *(Looking at his watch)* We should already be out the door and I for one— *(Finishing his drink)* —am ready to make the charge. *(He opens the door and gestures for her to lead the way out)*

ANGELA ...You didn't answer the question.

TOBY What question? I don't remember the question.

ANGELA Am I doing the right thing?

TOBY Angela, for God's sake, there is a garden filled with family and friends. A man you love is waiting—admittedly in pumps—to put a ring upon your finger. There is a cake the size of a caravan, several tons of sandwiches and an ocean's worth of boiled prawns. Now please tell me that four thousand crustaceans have not died in vain.

ANGELA moves to the chair upstage centre and sits down (on TOBY's mobile phone)

...Why are you sitting? Angela people are waiting. Remember—a door closing, another opening...? Here look, an open door, let's go for it!

TOBY walks out of the room and returns a few seconds later.

(referring to the whisky) Will I be needing another of these?

ANGELA What you forget, Toby, is that your greatest virtue has always been your greatest fault. Your remarkable, foolhardy and unique ability to always tell the truth. You were such a terrible liar. Ever since childhood. So you always said what you thought. A ridiculous concept in the modern world. Nobody tells the truth anymore. But still you insisted on it. It got you in trouble at school, it lost you several jobs, and I suspect, you forfeited several potential wives into the bargain. I learnt that if I ever needed the truth—you would be the one to ask.

TOBY But today isn't about me.

ANGELA Well, thank God for that—look at the suit you're
wearing.

TOBY Angela—

ANGELA Just—give me—

TOBY *looks at his watch.*

—Stop looking at your watch! I'm fed up of watches and
clocks and schedules and— It's all such a rush. Everything
these days is done in a panic. Nobody is at peace unless
they're out of breath roaring round a supermarket. I don't
want to run for any more buses, I don't want any more fast
food, I don't want to hurry—I want five minutes. I want
five minutes with nothing planned, nothing to do, nothing
to think about today, tomorrow, next week. Five minutes
without schedule. Can I have five minutes—please!

TOBY *(closing the door)* ...I'm sure we can arrange you five
minutes. We can be sure to organise that. But, may I
suggest—not this *particular* five minutes—let's find a
different five minutes. Trust me on this. I am your elder
brother and I—command it. Just trust in me this one time
and—get up on your feet, follow me next door, and let's get
this over with.

ANGELA "Get this over with"? This is supposed to be the most
romantic event of a woman's life. I don't want to "get it
over with".

TOBY It's a figure of speech.

ANGELA *(being pompous)* Well I don't much care for it.

TOBY Don't go all Jane Austen on me, not now. —Would it help
if I got you that coffee?

ANGELA It would help if you told me how you really feel about
this.

TOBY Why? What does it— *(He shrugs then he grabs a chair and goes over to sit beside her)* ...I am not in any way an expert on finding love. I would have thought that was obvious.

ANGELA What about Kristina? You loved Kristina.

TOBY I *liked* Kristina. I lived with Kristina, I spent hours in happy political debate with Kristina. But it was not—any kind of blossoming romance. All intellect, not enough passion.

ANGELA It could have been.

TOBY No—that would have required commitment. And that's not something I ...I see that more as *your* department. You like being married. You must do—you've done it often enough.

ANGELA *gives him a slap on his arm and they smirk at each other.*

...I wish Mum and Dad were still here. I wonder how they would have reacted to what we've become.

ANGELA I expect it would have killed them.

TOBY No. Not at all. They'd be very proud of you.

ANGELA You're wrong about that. I've made such a mess.

TOBY Admittedly, you have had your moments. But you bounce back. Like a giant trampoline.

ANGELA Don't look at the dress when you say that.

TOBY I wasn't. But I mean what I say—there's something to be admired in the way you persist and battle your way forward. People so often just give up. Resign themselves to a life living on their own or one at least without a hand to hold. But you don't accept that. You stay in the game. You refuse to not be hopeful. You keep looking.

ANGELA Maybe I look too hard...

TOBY *(cannot think of anything to add to that; kissing* **ANGELA** *on the cheek)* ...You still want that coffee?

ANGELA *nods that she does.*

(going into the kitchen and pouring **ANGELA** *a cup of coffee from the jug)* ...Sugar?

ANGELA Just three spoonfuls.

TOBY "Just" three...?

ANGELA I don't need to worry about my weight now. I'm already *in* the dress.

TOBY *(putting the sugars into her coffee)* Ah yes—the joy of being married. You can finally get really fat.

ANGELA You seem to manage that perfectly well without a ring on your finger.

TOBY But I never intend to get married—so the rules don't apply. *(He brings over* **ANGELA***'s coffee)*

ANGELA So that's it? Whatever happens in life, whoever you might meet, you're never going to have a wedding?

TOBY No. This is the last time I ever intend to be photographed standing next to anything "vanilla" ...Now drink up quickly and let's go. *(He turns again towards the door)*

As he does so, his mobile phone begins to ring—it plays a loud piercing tune. The shock of the noise, combined with the phone vibrating, causes **ANGELA** *to jump in shock—spilling her cup of coffee down the front of her wedding dress.*

ANGELA Oh God!! Oh my God!!

TOBY *(seeing what has happened and throwing his hands in the air in exasperation)* It's only my phone ringing—why such a bloody reaction?!

ANGELA I was sitting on it! It was also on vibrate!!

TOBY Why would you sit on someone's mobile?

ANGELA I didn't know I was sitting on it! Look at the size of this thing— *(Referring to her dress)* I'm half the room!

TOBY *(running across the room towards the bathroom)* I'll get a cloth.

TOBY *exits into the bathroom.*

The phone keeps playing its tune.

ANGELA Should I answer that?

TOBY *(from inside the bathroom)* No!! Don't touch anything!

TOBY *comes back with a damp cloth.*

(proceeding to wipe the coffee off the front of the dress) ...You and your bloody coffee.

ANGELA It was an accident—I'm on edge! ...Is it coming out?

TOBY It's coffee! It doesn't come out. All I can do is blend it in with the dress so it looks more like café au lait. *(He continues to work at the stain)*

ANGELA *(answering the phone)* Hallo?

TOBY Why are you answering that now?

ANGELA It's a phone, isn't it? That's what they're for! *(Into the phone)* Yes, I'm here—sorry? ...Yes, yes, we're on our way now. Just a few last minute adjustments... Oh, is it really? My watch must have stopped, I didn't realise we were late... Yes, we'll come down right this second... Oh yes—you could do that, yes. *(Ending the phone call)* Oh God, they're starting the music.

TOBY What is it— "Here comes the Bride" or "It's a long way to Tipperary"?

ANGELA *(referring to her dress front)* Can't we just remove that bit?

TOBY What?

ANGELA That bit of material. Just remove it.

TOBY How?

ANGELA Tear it, cut it. There's plenty of other material on this bloody monstrosity, we can afford to lose a yard or two. But one thing I do know is that I'm not parading down the aisle with Nescafe dribbling down my chest.

TOBY Well—have you any scissors?

ANGELA Sod the scissors—just tear it!

TOBY I can't do that, the fabric's all stitched together with—

ANGELA Oh for heaven's sake!!

Pushing **TOBY** *away, she shoves one half of the material into her mouth. Then, turning to face upstage, she puts a foot up onto a piece of furniture for support and then— with great force and a yell—tears off a section of the dress. A pause. She hands the piece of stained fabric to* **TOBY**.

TOBY Oh good, you got it.

ANGELA *then turns around to face downstage. She is holding a much larger section of material in her other hand. The entire front of her dress has been split open and she stands there in a dress with absolutely no chest area—revealing her breasts and a flowery bra.*

ANGELA I think I ripped too hard.

TOBY *puts his head in his hands.*

...Oh, Toby!

TOBY There's no need to panic. Let's just... Where on earth did you get that *awful* bra?!

ANGELA It was a present from Simon.

TOBY Well, he'll be delighted to see it so prominently on display.

ANGELA Do something!

TOBY What? I'm not a seamstress. Have you got a needle and thread?

ANGELA Why would I need a needle and thread? The dress came ready made.

TOBY We have to attach it back to the— What about safety pins?

ANGELA No.

TOBY Why don't you have a safety pin?

ANGELA I'm getting married, I had other things on my mind!

TOBY *(dialling a number on his mobile)* Aunty Babs will have something.

ANGELA We don't have time, they're playing the music.

TOBY You cannot go down there with those things flobbing about.

ANGELA They don't flobber! They gently bounce.

TOBY In that bra, I'm surprised they don't scream for mercy. *(Answering the phone)* Hello? ...It's Toby.

> **ANGELA** *checks in her purse for something she could use.*

We have a slight situation with the dress—we need pins... Yes, pins. Talk to Aunty Babs—she'll have something... Aunty Babs—she's on the front row looking like a three piece suite... Yes, just send her up.

ANGELA Wait—I've found something.

TOBY *(into the phone)* Hang on. *(To* **ANGELA***)* Are you sure?

ANGELA Two hairpins and some dental floss.

> **TOBY** *looks despairing.*

...*And* one safety pin. People have achieved a lot more in a crisis with a lot less.

TOBY All right. *(Into the phone)* It's OK, we've found something. We'll be there in a minute—two minutes. *(He ends the phone call. He then takes the pins and dental floss and begins to fix*

*the dress – if he keeps his actions hidden from the audience,
then the dress could actually be re-fixed with velcro)* ...This is
why people get married in hotels and not in their neighbours'
garden. So there are members of staff and wedding planners
on hand to deal with unexpected circumstances.

ANGELA I found the pin, didn't I?!

TOBY At least you don't have too far to walk in the dress. Just
keep the flobbing—sorry, bouncing—to a minimum, please.

ANGELA Maybe this is just a bad omen.

TOBY Stop it.

ANGELA A sign. Is this a sign? Maybe it's just not right—falling
in love for the third time. Third-time love—isn't that an
oxymoron?

TOBY Oxy, no. Moron, possibly.

ANGELA I mean, am I just kidding myself? Making a fool of
myself?

TOBY *(finishing mending the dress and stepping back to view
it)* There—done.

ANGELA I still look like a giant snowball.

TOBY You do not. You look like a giant blancmange. Now will
it hold?

ANGELA *(checking it)* I think so.

TOBY Good. Crisis averted.

ANGELA Or just the first day of the crisis.

TOBY Well—always keep your dental floss handy. Are we going
now?

ANGELA But I didn't get my coffee.

TOBY What!

ANGELA I wanted a coffee—I needed a coffee.

TOBY You *had* a coffee.

ANGELA My *chest* had a coffee, my dress had a coffee—I got sod all.

TOBY I'm afraid now you'll just have to wait till after the ceremony. *(He heads towards the door)*

ANGELA No, no, no—I need the—I want the caffeine. I haven't had any all day, I'll get a headache.

TOBY Well, that'll come in handy for the honeymoon.

ANGELA Toby—

TOBY No! No more hot beverages for you, young lady. Simon is waiting. They're all waiting. Now—do as you're told! *(He opens the door and points out of it)*

ANGELA *sits down.*

Angela! Angela... Angela? Oh dear Lord... *(He closes the door)* I should have had a brother... Coffee?

ANGELA That's all I want.

TOBY Fine. *(He goes into the kitchen and pours another cup of coffee. He adds the sugar by simply pouring a mass of it straight out of the bag and into the cup. He brings the drink back to* **ANGELA** *without stirring it, then goes over to the window and leans out of it, looking across to the neighbouring garden)* They're all still there... Though you can't expect people to wait forever.

ANGELA *doesn't respond, but just sips her coffee.* **TOBY**'s *mobile rings again.*

...Ask not for whom the bell tolls...! *(Answering the phone)* Yes—we're coming, we're coming! *(Ending the call)* ...Well?

ANGELA *finishes her coffee in one gulp.*

...Feeling better?

ANGELA I have no idea... I just feel—swamped by all the bad omens.

TOBY You just spilt coffee. Don't confuse omens with incompetence. Angela—we really have to go! Right now! So winch yourself onto your feet and head west. *(Helping* **ANGELA** *stand up and walking her to the door)* Hey! You're getting married—don't forget to smile. *(He opens the door and then puts a hand on* **ANGELA***'s back to encourage her forward)*

ANGELA *(resisting* **TOBY***'s pushing)* Don't push me.

TOBY I'm not pushing you, I'm encouraging you.

ANGELA Stop it!

> **TOBY** *stops pushing.*

...It's all right—I'll go. I can do this.

TOBY Yes—you absolutely can. Just take a deep breath.

> **ANGELA** *stretches herself to her full height—takes a deep breath—and leaves, with the aid of an extra shove from* **TOBY***.*

> **TOBY** *sighs with relief and exasperation. He checks the room, grabs his keys and his mobile and heads towards the door. But just as he does so, the stage is struck by a flash of lightning and a loud clap of thunder. A sudden burst of rain is seen through the window, pouring down violently.*

> **TOBY** *freezes at the door, overcome with disbelief. He rushes over to the window and looks out examining the torrential rain.*

> **ANGELA** *enters. She is soaked to the skin, her hair has collapsed onto her face and water drips from every inch of her. The front of the dress has come undone again and she is one big soggy mess.*

> **TOBY** *turns to see her and screams in horror.*

ANGELA It's raining...!

TOBY OK, OK—there's no need to panic.

ANGELA Why not? I would have thought this was the perfect time to panic.

TOBY I'll get some towels.

> **TOBY** *runs into the bedroom.*

ANGELA *(looking at herself in the mirror)* My hair has collapsed... Even the rotten bra is soaked.

> **TOBY** *returns with two towels.*

TOBY It's all right. Rather than a white wedding, we'll have a—*wet* wedding. *(Starting to dry* **ANGELA***'s hair)* ...It'll be fine. Everybody brought umbrellas, in case of this.

ANGELA It's ruined.

TOBY Not at all! Rain can be very romantic. Kisses in the rain, walks in the rain...making love in the rain.

ANGELA You make love in the *rain*? You should see a therapist.

TOBY Dry your own breasts, or we'll *both* need therapists.

> **ANGELA** *dries her chest area with the other towel as* **TOBY** *continues drying her hair.*

ANGELA ...I should have known something bad would happen. I saw two black cats on the road on the way here.

TOBY But that's *good* luck.

ANGELA They'd both been run over! *(Looking towards the window)* ...What's everyone doing out there?

TOBY I don't know.

ANGELA Well—look!

> **TOBY** *goes to the window and looks out. The rain is calming down.*

TOBY They've all got their umbrellas up. Aunty Babs is using her shoulder pads to shelter several small children. The food is being moved inside. It's all—it's all under control. *(Turning to* **ANGELA***)* It's just a bit of rain. I know everybody wants their wedding day to be perfect—

ANGELA I wasn't asking for "perfect". At this stage, I'd settle for catastrophic.

> **TOBY** *returns to* **ANGELA***'s side and looks at her hair. The excessive towelling has left it shooting up and out in all directions.*

TOBY What can we do with your hair? You look like you've just been plugged in.

ANGELA It took me hours. I put delicate little flowers in it.

TOBY ...What about the veil? Didn't the dress come with a veil?

ANGELA I wasn't going to wear it. I thought it would make me look stupid.

TOBY *(staring wide-eyed at the mess of hair)* ...I'll get the veil. Where is it?

ANGELA In the bedroom cupboard.

> **TOBY** *runs into the bedroom.*

—But it would be easier to cancel!

TOBY *(from the bedroom)* No cancellations. Not on my watch! We'll just rise to the challenge.

ANGELA I'm very wet. I'm going to catch a cold.

> **TOBY** *returns with the veil.*

TOBY So, catch a cold. Your new husband can look after you. Feed you chicken soup and hot lemon— *(Fixing the veil onto her head)* —and you can reflect on how lucky you are to be married. *(Pulling the veil down over* **ANGELA***'s face)* ...There—that's much better. We can't see your face at all.

ANGELA Oh charming!

TOBY I meant from the point of view that your make-up is all smudged. And it covers your hair beautifully. Success!

ANGELA Oh Toby...

TOBY No—don't give me, "Oh Toby". We are handling this upset brilliantly... Umbrella?

ANGELA I don't know!

TOBY I saw it earlier... Wait! I know. (*He goes into the kitchen and locates the umbrella there. He opens it up to check it is working*)

ANGELA Don't open it! That's bad luck!

TOBY Will you just stop it with all that. (*He takes the umbrella over to* **ANGELA**)

ANGELA Close the bloody thing will you—it's very bad karma. (*She fights over the umbrella with him*)

TOBY Only *you* could reference Buddhism at a catholic ceremony.

ANGELA Close it.

TOBY Leave it alone, would you. We're going now. Leave it as it is.

ANGELA No! You have to—

Their scuffle over the umbrella causes them to knock over the mirror. It falls forward onto the floor with a loud crash of breaking glass.

Oh my God!! That's seven years bad—

TOBY Stop it! Stop it!!

ANGELA We broke the—

TOBY I know we broke the... But don't give it any deep meaning.

ANGELA I broke a mirror the weekend before my first marriage— and look what happened.

TOBY Well that proves it's all rubbish. A broken mirror is meant to bring *seven* years bad luck. The marriage only lasted five!

ANGELA *bursts into tears.*

...Oh, don't! ...Don't cry. You'll get all snotty. Come on, now... Have you got a tissue?

She proceeds to blow her nose on a section of her wedding dress. She then hangs her head low and looks about to collapse.

Angela... Listen...listen to me. *(Taking hold of both of* **ANGELA***'s hands)* There are no omens, good or bad—just feelings of uncertainty about something and looking for some mysterious force to point you in the right direction. At the end of the day, you have to make your own decisions and not blame it on the heavens. And maybe you'll do the right thing and maybe the wrong thing—but you take that chance and you—follow your heart... Angela—someone wants to marry you. To be with you your whole life—or in your case, for as long as possible. I can't tell you what's going to happen. But right now—there's an opportunity to *see* what happens. To roll the dice—and see if you get lucky. *(Lifting the veil from her face and using his fingers wipes the tears from her eyes)* ...You know, the thing I always admired about you is your bravery. I've never had the guts to do this. Oh, they say I've just never found the right girl, but...we know that's not the reason. I just think about having to make a promise to someone and keep it—and it scares me... So my wish today is that one of us *isn't* scared. That we're not both fighting through this world alone... I'll tell you the *truth*—that's a horrible dress. And it's horrible weather. And I think the buffet may have been created by someone with two fingers and a death wish... But the one thing here that is perfect—is the atmosphere of *hope*... That's all we can ask for.

A moment. It stops raining outside.

ANGELA *(her face brightening at this)* ...It's stopped raining.

TOBY Come on, Angela. It's time one of us got married...again.

> **ANGELA** *nods.* **TOBY** *points her to the door and she wedding marches towards it, as we hear the music "**HERE COMES THE BRIDE**" in the background.*

> **ANGELA** *exits.*

> **TOBY** *watches her go, filled with pride. Suddenly, there is another flash of lightning and a roll of thunder.*

> *(looking upwards, as though speaking to the heavens)* ... Oh shut up!

> *He exits, shutting the door behind him.*

> *Snap blackout.*

The End

FURNITURE AND PROPERTY LIST

ACT I, Duet I – Blind Date

On stage: Kitchen. *In it:* Fridge, glasses, orange juice, vodka
            bottle
           Photo of **Jonathan**
           Cabinet. *In it:* trophy, decanters and glasses
           Phone
           Jonathan's jacket

Personal: **Jonathan:** ginger toupée, wallet
           Wendy: glasses, mobile phone

Offstage: Dating magazine, block of cheese (**Wendy**)

ACT I, Duet II – Secretarial Skills

On stage: Wedding cake, with ceramic figurines on top, in a
           cake box
           Champagne *(for drinking)*
           Glasses
           Knife
           Plates
           Bottles of champagne around the room
           Phone
           Sofa *(moveable)*
           Mirror
           Bottle of Perrier water
           Chairs
           Diary

Offstage: Ornate pill box. *In it:* pill (**Janet**)

Personal: **Janet:** earrings
           Barrie: cigarettes and lighter

ACT I, Duet III – The Holiday

On stage: Sofa. *On it:* a removeable coloured throw
Kitchen. *In it:* Crisps, a jar of olives *(edible)*
Bobby's spare pair of shoes
Harry Potter book
Packet of digestive biscuits *(edible)*
Bottle of perfume

Offstage: Cocktail complete with umbrella, etc. suitcase, pile
of clothes (**Bobby**)
Cocktail, Bobby's pyjamas, pair of Mickey Mouse
slippers (**Shelley**)
Business card, huge cocktail, empty olive jar (**Stage
Manager**)

Personal: **Shelley:** watch

ACT I, Duet IV – The Bride-To-Be

On stage: Bunches of flowers and wrapped gifts
Chair
Angela's purse *in it:* hairpins, a safety pin, and dental
floss
Kitchen. *In it:* tissues, coffee jug, coffee cup, bag
of sugar, spoon, umbrella, kitchen cupboard. *In
it:* bottle of whisky, glasses
Mirror

Offstage: Damp cloth, two towels, wedding veil (**Toby**)

Personal: **Toby:** watch, mobile phone

LIGHTING PLOT

ACT I, Duet I – Blind Date

Practical fitting required: nil
1 interior. The same scene throughout

To open: General interior lighting

Cue 1   **Jonathan** leaves and **Wendy** follows,
          closing the door behind her   (Page 18)
          Lights fade to blackout

ACT I, Duet II – Secretarial Skills

Practical fitting required: nil
1 interior. The same scene throughout

To open: General interior lighting

Cue 2   **Barrie** and **Janet** give each other
          a quick peck of kiss   (Page 38)
          Blackout

Act II, Duet III – The Holiday

Practical fitting required: nil
1 interior. The same scene throughout

To open: General interior lighting

Cue 3   A knock on the door. **Bobby** opens
          the door   (Page 41)
          Party lights beyond

Cue 4   Another knock on the door.   (Page 43)
          Party lights beyond

ACT II, Duet IV – The Bride-To-Be

Practical fitting required: nil
1 interior. The same scene throughout

To open: General interior lighting

EFFECTS PLOT

ACT I, Duet I – Blind Date

ACT I, Duet II – Secretarial Skills

ACT II, Duet III – The Holiday

VISIT THE SAMUEL FRENCH BOOKSHOP AT THE ROYAL COURT THEATRE

Browse plays and theatre books, get expert advice and enjoy a coffee

Samuel French Bookshop
Royal Court Theatre
Sloane Square
London
SW1W 8AS
020 7565 5024

Shop from thousands of titles on our website

 samuelfrench.co.uk

 samuelfrenchltd

 samuel french uk

Lightning Source UK Ltd.
Milton Keynes UK
UKHW020628170319
339280UK00004B/19/P